MW01235747

A MOTLEY CREW

How Jesus Turned Ordinary Men into Dynamic Disciples

Dr. Sam Warren

ISBN 978-1-0980-5946-0 (paperback)
ISBN 978-1-0980-5947-7 (digital)

Copyright © 2020 by Dr. Sam Warren

Christian Faith Publishing, Inc.
832 Park Avenue
Meadville, PA 16335
www.christianfaithpublishing.com

Printed in the United States of America

ENDORSEMENTS

In the ever-changing world of the modern pastor, my friend Sam Warren has provided some much-needed help. This book blends biblical teaching with practical help that will bring encouragement to pastors. You will want to keep this book close at hand and refer to it often as you serve the Lord in His church.

—**Dr. David Butts**
Chairman of America's National
Prayer Committee
Founder and President of Harvest
Prayer Ministries

I have known author Dr. Sam Warren for almost forty years, and for over ten of those years, we worked together in the same denomination offices, where I came to understand how near and dear the local pastorate vocation is to his heart. So it is no surprise that, as a writer, he recorded his passions in this study.

Sam explores the day-to-day biblical mandate of the local church, giving special attention to the leadership, which includes the pastor along with the elders and deacons. This study includes the process of asking some very practical questions:

- *What is a pastor to do when he realizes that the way things have been done are in contradiction to the teaching of the Bible?*
- *If those who make up the church don't know why we exist, how will anyone else?*

- *Is the preaching within our local churches appropriate for the equipping of the saints to do the work of the ministry?*
- *What would happen if the church was actively engaging the people in their neighborhood, workplace, leisure sites, and anywhere else they go in such a way that would lead them to faith in Christ?*
- *How does a pastor begin to make certain that the truths of the Scriptures are passed on to the next generation?*

In discussion of these questions and others, Sam uses many illustrations—some personal—to examine God's purpose and plan for building a biblically healthy church, which moves beyond information to transformation. As the church of today struggles to be relevant in our present society, it is surmised that the contents of this study will be helpful to local pastors, along with the local church leadership, as a valuable resource for making disciples and fulfilling the Great Commission.

—Pamela L. Buchanan
Former ACGC coordinator
of Women's Ministries

I hear an echo as I read this book: the voice of a teacher of teachers. I've had the privilege of hearing Dr. Sam share many of these truths in the past in churches where I've served, as well as in leadership events I've hosted for pastors throughout Africa (Namibia, Liberia, and Kenya). His heart to see the truths of 2 Timothy 2:2 become the heart of pastors everywhere has never changed. It's heartening to know that Sam has finally put to writing much of this life message he has so faithfully learned and taught.

—Rev. Frank R. Jewett
Pastor, Advent Christian
Church of Haverhill, Massachusetts
First area director for Africa and Europe
Advent Christian World Missions

Sam has done a great job of taking a complex question and making it very simple. I'd highly encourage any church leadership to read this book and take time discussing each chapter. I know it will stimulate great thought and provide some fresh and new insight. I highly commend this book to you.

—Dr. Dann Spader
Founder of Sonlife and Global Youth Initiative
Author of 4 *Chair Discipling*

When you think of church, what do you think of, and what do you expect? For years I had a view of the church based on traditions formed over time that sadly, I believe, have strayed away from the original design. This book lovingly guides the reader into an understanding of the original design of the church and why it exists. Christ established His church for a very specific reason.

Dr. Warren lays out Christ's design and plan for His church in a way that is not only informative but also exciting. Through Dr. Warren's teaching, I have gained a fresh understanding of the true mission of the church and in the process, developed a closer walk with Jesus. I have had the privilege of having Dr. Warren's help in guiding me and the church I pastor. He has become such a dear friend, brother, and mentor to me. He has encouraged me immensely in God's Word, and the blessings that have resulted are immeasurable.

The biblical teachings that he imparts relationally are carefully and lovingly documented in this book in such a way that it captured my attention from the very beginning and held it throughout. It has been a great blessing to fully realize my purpose as a follower of Christ and our purpose collectively as His church. We are here to be disciples who make disciples.

If you want your life to have an impact on others and your church to have an impact on your community for Christ Jesus, this book is for you. I believe it is time we return to be the church Jesus intends for us to be. I pray that His Holy Spirit will guide you, and that God will bless you as you read this book.

—Rev. Randy Henderson
Pastor, Ephesus Advent Christian Church

Dr. Sam Warren is a treasure. His gentle style, his forthright insight, his practical and constructive advice is a welcome voice to the world of church consultants and coaches. Reading his book, you are made aware of his acquaintance with experts in the field, his own experience, and exposure to the theory and dynamics of a healthy congregation; and yet one is not overwhelmed. The style is simple and straightforward conversational. It's boots on the ground advice. I commend Sam, his book, and his expertise to any congregation.

—Dr. Doug Small
CCU and founder of Project Pray
Author of over twenty books

Dr. Sam Warren's book is a practical and handy exposition of the methodology that Jesus and the Apostle Paul used to train their disciples, not only in how to live lives that would be pleasing to God, but also how to train others who would go on to train yet others to do the same. If the church that Jesus founded had been following the principles that are spelled out in this book for the past twenty centuries, both the church and the world would be in much better shape (spiritually, at least) than they are today. Sadly, these concepts have been pretty much buried under a large pile of mostly useless habits, formats, and traditions that have proved almost impossible to get out from under. But there is good news! It's not too late to start a quiet revolution, and, believe it or not, God can use YOU to do it. You don't have to be a trained theologian either to understand how or to put these principles into practice. You don't even have to be a professional minister; all you need is an open mind and a willing heart. Give it a try!

Once in a while, you stumble over gold nuggets that someone else has mined, and they share them with you. This book is that experience. It is presented in such a way that any shepherd could gather and grow his flock. It would be hard to miss the mark of spiritual growth with this book. It is a powerful diagnostic tool and equally powerful biblical plan for remedy.

Critical to addressing the issue of institutional, irrelevant church in our day is a return to the first century priority of making disciples who make disciples. Dr. Warren's reflections on this motley crew, who turned the world upside down for Jesus, is a timely resource for our day.

To my wife, Shelly. Your love to me, support of our family, and faithfulness to the Lord have sustained me through our life together. Thank you from the bottom of my heart for your belief in me and encouragement in the writing of this book.

CONTENTS

INTRODUCTION

You live and learn. At any rate, you live.

—Douglas Adams

Perhaps I'm a slow learner. You would think that something so important would become clear after forty-plus years of experience in the life of the local church. However, it's not uncommon for pastors to get so involved in the work of the church that spending time trying to change things gets set to the side due to the amount of work needing to get done. One author has called this the "tyranny of the urgent."[1]

The demands placed upon us can come from within or from those around us. Quite often, the demands are present simply because that's the way it's always been done, and no one has recognized that things must change. To question or propose the thought of changing the way things are done in the church can be met with an enormous amount of resistance. However, what is a pastor to do when he realizes that the way things have been done are in contradiction to the teaching of the Bible?

I have personally struggled with this dilemma many times over the past forty years. I have been faced with resistance to the suggestion that the church is off the mark in terms of how it is living out biblical truth in so many ways. To suggest that the church is wrong

---

[1]. Charles Hummel, *Tyranny of the Urgent* (PO Box, Downers Grove, IL 60515, 1967).

in the way it is doing something is for many an attack on their ancestors, previous pastors, and leaders who established the church and have led it for years. Let's be honest, a pastor entering a new pastorate is inheriting a world of rules, ideas, traditions, and more that may or may not be acceptable to him as he begins to lead his new ministry. The church called him because he seemed nice, and he preached a "good" sermon on his candidating weekend, but in only a few years, provided he survives, the church has a new list of beliefs and practices that are being formed and followed by those who make up the church. These, too, will be hard to change, if needed.

At some point in time, one would hope for a pastor to come along who is willing to stay long enough to make significant changes in the church for the good. Changes that are designed to lead the church toward biblical health. My experience working with local churches gives me enough evidence to know that this type of pastor is rare. For those who long for the church to be healthy, there is significant reason to be concerned.

WHAT WENT WRONG?

I can remember clearly the things that were taught in my pastoral ministry course in college and what was not taught as well. For example, I was never taught how pastors were treated differently in the eyes of the IRS and what that meant for those in ministry. I was not taught how to do a funeral service or how to conduct a wedding. No one told me that I would be a counselor; yet many in the church today expect the pastor to be somewhat of an expert in areas of life that we have no understanding, and we sit for hours listening and advising people what to do.

While there is much to be thankful for when it comes to being part of a local church, over time, the culture of the church can become self-serving. That is, it's more about what the church does for me rather than how the church is equipping me to fulfil Christ's mandate to reach the lost and turn them into disciples who make disciples (Matt. 28).

Pastors are burdened with a host of responsibilities that have little to do with equipping people for the work of the ministry (Eph. 4). Perhaps they don't believe this to be a priority, or more likely the church's infrastructure will not allow them to pursue this mandate in all that they do. If this is the condition of the local church, it is no wonder that churches are dying or on the brink of losing any kind of significant impact on those they serve.

When visiting people regularly and preaching a sermon every Sunday is the most common expectation of a pastor, it is no surprise that the church is so dysfunctional today. Imagine a church that looks for a pastor who can meet these expectations but is void of understanding the most basic truths put forth in the Bible concerning the purpose and practices of the church, and you will get the picture of most churches in the twenty-first century. To argue that there is a need to reshape the heart and mind of the church today will not be received well by many but absolutely necessary if the church is going to fulfill the mandate given to the first disciples (Matt. 28:16–20).

TO CHANGE OR NOT TO CHANGE?

For some, the idea that the church has to change, especially as we go forward into the twenty-first century is a surprise. One would think that after two thousand years since the church was established, we would have gotten it right. The belief and conviction to argue for change is even more difficult knowing that I have contributed to the dysfunction of the local church for a long time. Perhaps you've done the same.

If you are reading this book, it will be hard to give serious thought to the ideas I will share. It will be almost impossible because I know you love your local church. And some of you have been part of your church for most, if not all of your life. The thought that you might have had it all wrong is too much to consider. Worse than that, believing that something's not right but having done little or nothing to bring about biblical health is, as they say, "a hard pill to swallow." However, I want to say, "It's never too late to be right especially when it comes to knowing Christ and the purpose of his church" (Matt. 28).

Sadly, statistics show that hundreds of churches are closing or dying every year. One might ask why. Could it be that they are dying because they don't even know why they exist and how they are supposed to function? When the church doesn't grow, one is compelled to ask why. It is the most important question a pastor, and his leadership team must ask. If you are willing to explore this question and what it means for the local church, read on. In this book, we will explore many of the reasons for the church's twenty-first century's dysfunctional condition and consider what the Bible teaches that can move us toward health.

FINDING THE RIGHT PATH

The right path is the one that leads to the right conclusion. If the goal of the church is to make disciples who make disciples, one might truly question whether or not the church of today is on the right path. Some have suggested that the church should increase by at least 10 percent conversion rate per year when it is healthy. Unfortunately, most churches grow in conversion growth by a mere 2 percent or less. Add to this the fact that most churches do little to help new believers move toward maturity, leading to a greater level of dysfunction for church members and resulting in another contributing factor to the lack of health in the church.

In the following pages, the reader will be confronted with thoughts, concepts, and even proposals for the church. Thoughts about the contemporary health of the church, concepts expressing the original intent for the church, and how those concepts can be expressed in and through the ministry of today's church. Finally, in what might seem to be bold, one will find proposals on how the church might revisit God's purpose and plan for building a biblically healthy church. Subjects such as purpose, prayer, leadership, strategic planning, worship, missions, evangelism, purposeful programming, and more will find their way into our discussion. I have included a study guide for each chapter that will enable any pastor or leader to further discuss and apply these thoughts to the ones under their care. I would love to have you join me in this journey. If you are so inclined, *please read on*!

CHAPTER 1

STARTING WITH WHY

Going to church doesn't make you a Christian any more
than going to a garage makes you an automobile.

—Billy Sunday

When it comes to fast food, hamburgers have met their match. You
know what I am talking about, especially if you have eaten at least
once at Chick-fil-A. Their food is great, but the experience one has
at Chick-fil-A goes far beyond the food. The minute you walk in and
even before you get out of your car, there is evidence that they are
expecting you. It's hard not to notice that the people who work at
Chick-fil-A care about much more than giving you a meal.

One day, while getting ready to order my lunch at Chick-fil-A,
the conversation took a humorous turn when I responded to the
young girl taking my order by saying that it was *my pleasure* to meet
her. Unexpectedly, and suddenly, her eyes got big, and her body language changed as she leaned toward me and whispered these words:
"Are you one of us?"

I responded by saying, "I don't know. Who are you?"

Obviously, the people who work for Chick-fil-A have been
trained to say this phrase to their customers in every situation, but
it reveals much more than the fact that they listened during their
training. If you listen closely and hear it enough, you realize it reveals

nothing about *what* they do (cook and serve food) but *why* (with a heart of serving) they do it. The organization knows that once a person hears this phrase and says it enough, something begins to happen in the mind of the person saying it.

Once, while teaching a seminary course on the topic of teams and team building, I decided to bring in the local manager of Chick-fil-A to share with the class his thoughts on functioning like a healthy team. He had some amazing things to share on how they go about building a team. The class knew that the shared principles worked because we had all eaten at Chick-fil-A and seen it in action. The discussion we had was great, especially since he brought lunch when he arrived; and yes, when we thanked him for his generosity of time and food, he simply said, "My pleasure!"

While the manager offered some amazing insights into what Chick-fil-A does to build effective teams, the biggest surprise and impact came from his comments on the culture of the organization by telling us that Chick-fil-A is *not a Christian organization.* As the gasps were calming down from the students, he continued to say, "Chick-fil-A is an organization that lives by biblical principles." We took that to mean that their work is not so much about **what** they do but **why** they do it.

According to Simon Sinek, author of the book *Start with Why,* "very few people or companies can clearly articulate WHY they do WHAT they do. When I say WHY, I don't mean to make money—that's the result. By WHY I mean what is your purpose, cause or belief? Why do you get out of bed every morning?[2] And WHY should anyone care? From a business point of view, people don't buy WHAT you do, they buy WHY you do it."[3]

Sinek continues by saying that "if a company does not have a clear sense of the WHY then it is impossible for the outside world to perceive anything more than WHAT the company does."[4] Years ago,

---

[2]   Simon Sinek, *Start with Why: How Great Leaders Inspire Everyone to Take Action* (Portfolio/Penguin, 375 Hudson Street, New York, NY 10014, 2009), pg. 39.

[3]   Ibid., pg. 39.

[4]   Ibid., pg. 64.

while serving as a pastor of a local church, I posed the question about the thousands of people who drove by our facility every day and wondered what they thought about us. Do they know WHY we are a church in their community, or is it possible that the only clue they have is the WHAT they see us doing? If they ever connect with us as a church, it may only be due to the fact that WHAT we did somehow crossed their path. The problem is they may never know WHY we exist and why we do WHAT we do. *The real question becomes:* "If those who make up the church don't know why we exist, how will anyone else?"

CHURCH GROWTH?

For years, people have studied the dynamics of church growth. Perspectives on this topic are many, and one would think with the exhaustive presence of churches, essentially on every corner in the cities of our country in both urban and rural contexts, the impact would be seen on a greater scale. There is no doubt that the expansion of the church's presence can be seen, but one might wonder if it's making any difference. We know what is happening when we see churches sprouting up everywhere; however, do we know why they are doing it and what they are hoping, even praying, will happen as a result of their presence?

It's not surprising that the average passerby might not know why the church is showing up in their neighborhood. They can see that there is now a church building where there was only an empty field before, but what **is** surprising and, in fact, troubling is that most people who are members of these churches know what they are dong (building a church facility), but they don't know **why** it is being done. In simple terms, mast churches have not wrestled with **why** *the* **what** *is being done.* Why are we making the effort to build a church and place it in a new community? Are we planning to do the same thing that we have done all along? Will the *what* change as we are guided by the *why* of our existence? What if we don't know the why? Where does that leave the church?

WHEN *WHAT* IS NOT ENOUGH

Churches are interesting communities of faith. Most are characterized by their love for God and their desire to worship him; yet quite often, they fall short of carrying out the mandate given by Christ to his disciples.

Jesus expected his followers to leave the confines of their buildings to engage people with the life-changing message of Christ. Most churches focus on getting people to come to the church building in hopes that being around believers, and especially their preacher, they will somehow experience a spiritual *osmosis.*

This approach sounds good, but when we look carefully at the nature of the church, we see that Jesus never told people to go to church. The reason is clear when one accepts the biblical idea that the church is people and not a building. At the heart of the great and everyday commission (Matt. 28:16–20), we see that the disciples are commanded to make disciples *as they go.*

THE GOSPEL OF LOVE

The call for Christians to love others is a message I have heard most of my life. The Scriptures bear witness to this in so many places but perhaps no more powerfully than in the writings of the Apostle John, who declares that our commitment to love in this world will be matched with confidence on the day of judgement:

> So, we have come to know and to believe the love
> that God has for us. God is love, and whoever
> abides in love abides in God and God abides in
> him. By this is love perfected with us, so that we
> may have confidence for the day of judgement,
> because as he is so also are, we in the world. (1
> John 4:16–17)

And yet this is not the way many non-Christians view believers. In the year 2007, David Kinnaman and Gabe Lyons conducted a study which revealed that *Christians are often perceived as hypocritical, insensitive and judgmental.*[5] A believer is one who understands and believes the love God has for us and experiences the reciprocal nature of God's love.

> God is love, and whoever abides in love abides
> in God, and God abides in him. (1 John 4:16b)

To say that you love people is not enough; one must actually demonstrate their love in tangible acts. No doubt this is what John wanted to communicate when he stated, "Little children, let us not love in word or talk, but indeed and in truth (1 John 3:18). The charge to love, the motivation to love, and the power to love is summarized in one final statement given by John: "We love because he first loved us" (1 John 4:19).

This is the WHY of Christian ministry in the world today. Churches are not built to simply house believers, outreach programs are not provided because we have a lot of resources, benevolent ministries are not offered because we are such kind people. *No, not at all.* We do all these things because *He first loved us, and we are to do the same.*

The challenge for local churches is not that we don't know the *what* of ministry. The challenge is to know *why* we do it and how that's the most important thing of all. The strategic approach to becoming the church that Christ wanted begins by answering the question of why we exist and why God has placed us in a particular place. Once the church figures this out, it can now discover HOW it is going to do it, and this is where we now turn our attention to.

---

5. David Kinnaman and Gabe Lyons, *unChristian: What a New Generation Really Thinks about Christianity...and Why It Matters* (Baker Book Publishing Company, Ada, MI, 2007).

CHAPTER 2

STRATEGICALLY EQUIPPING

However beautiful the strategy, you should
occasionally look at the results.

—Sir Winston Churchill

They used to call us PKs (you know, preacher's kid). I didn't know what it meant when I was young, but I came to realize that it wasn't always used in a favorable manner. Sometimes, it was used to suggest that I received special treatment simply because I was a PK. All I knew was that I lived in a family with a loving mom and dad and two sisters.

As the years went by and I was growing into a being a teenager, the fact that my dad was a pastor of a church never bothered me. In fact, I was proud of my dad even though I didn't really know what he did. For all I knew, he stood up in front of people on Sunday and a few other days during the week and talked about God. While my friends had dads who were teachers, electricians, farmers, and car salesmen, my dad was a preacher.

The fact that my father was a preacher at a local church is one thing, but understanding what that meant is quite another. I don't really know when I finally understood what it is that a pastor does. My only clue for many years was my experience as a preacher's son, and it was not until I attended a Bible college that I gained a deeper level of insight; yet even this proved to be inadequate.

A SURE FOUNDATON

Having grown up in a small denomination, I was not surprised for me to discover that many of our churches were small and being led by men that loved God, and meant well, but had never had any type of training in the exegesis of Scripture. For a people who believe that the Word of God is central to understanding what it means to love God and follow his commands, this is alarming. Shouldn't we be concerned about preaching that cannot achieve the most important thing ever delivered to Christ's disciples, which was to teach His followers to obey everything that He had commanded them (Matt. 28:16–20)?

This situation is made worse when preaching is the primary thing that a church looks for when calling a new pastor. They want to know if he can preach and, in most cases, "Can he preach sermons that I like?" In many situations, if he can't preach, the church won't call him. However, this doesn't seem to be all that common for the simple reason that most men who are seeking to pastor a church—even they—can preach one sermon that sounds good to most folks. The real question is whether or not the preaching is appropriate for the equipping of the saints to do the work of the ministry.

THE GOAL OF PREACHING

In response, people will say that all they want is for a preacher to preach the Gospel. Even preachers know that you can't spend all of your time preaching about the Gospel on a weekly basis because that's not the purpose of preaching. My brother-in-law, who is a preacher, once said that "if someone gets saved in his church, it will be by accident." No, he wasn't against it happening, and if it did, he would rejoice. Rather, he was speaking this way because this is not the purpose of the church. We, in the church, are not called to get people saved over and over again in the church gathering (as if that can happen). Rather, we are called to share the gospel with the lost and work to move them toward becoming fully developed disciples of Christ. In the church, this begins with biblical preaching, but our greatest success will be seen when the church becomes known for making disciples who make disciples.

This is why preaching is so important and central to what a preacher does and why it is important for a church to understand what God wants to accomplish through the church. The apostle Paul had a keen sense of the importance of the Word of God. He instructed the Ephesian Christians to take up the "the sword of the Spirit, which is the Word of God" (Eph. 6:17). Later, Paul shared this final challenge to young Timothy as he led the Ephesian church in Paul's stead:

> I charge you in the presence of God and of Christ Jesus, who is to judge the living and the dead, and by his appearing and his kingdom: **preach the word**; be ready in season and out of season; reprove, rebuke, and exhort, with complete patience and teaching. For the time is coming when people will not endure sound teaching but having itching ears, they will accumulate for themselves teachers to suit their own passions and will turn away from listening to the truth and wander off into myths. As for you, always be sober-minded, endure suffering, do the work of an evangelist, fulfill your ministry. (2 Tim. 4:1–5)

It is clear from this text that preaching is more than preaching the gospel. According to Paul, the work of the pastor/teacher is to **equip** the saints for the work of the ministry (Eph. 4:11–12). The real condition of everyone who becomes a part of the church is made clear in these words, which suggest that each new believer falls short of what God wants and needs in order for the church to fulfill His mandate.

The idea of being **equipped** is seen in the New Testament's use of the word *mending* in "mending a net" (Matt. 4:21) and here in Paul's letter to the Ephesian believers (Eph. 4:11), where the role of the pastor/teacher is to *mend* or *equip* the saints for the work of the ministry.[6] In simple terms, the believer is *mended* or *equipped* through the work of the Holy Spirit and the Word of God to bring every believer to the point of being able to fulfill God's mandate for the church, which is to make disciples who make disciples (Matt. 28:16–20). All of this is achieved in and through a healthy and unified church body when each and every joint (believer) who is nourished by Christ does its part. When this happens, the church grows (Eph. 4:16b). This growth spoken of by the Apostle Paul begins with the pastor/teacher,[7] equipping each believer in such a way that they pursue and reach maturity. As each believer grows in faith and is connected[8] (knee bone connected to the thigh bone) to another believer in the body, the church becomes stable and grows.

A NEW KIND OF LEADER

One can only imagine how many times the Apostle Paul found himself sitting in a prison, thinking about what it would take to enable the churches he planted to grow. He often started his letters to the churches with statements of thanksgiving for the tremendous service being rendered by the saints as they carried on the work of the ministry:

> We give thanks to God always for all of you, constantly mentioning you in our prayers, remembering before our God and Father your works of faith and labor of love and steadfastness of hope in our Lord Jesus Christ. (1 Thess. 1:2–3)

Part of Paul's joy and thankful spirit came from that the fact that he had men whom he had equipped to help in the expansion of the ministry that he was having with the churches. It is clear that Paul believed in the development of leadership as evidenced by his invest-

---

6. Καταρτιζοντασ ανδ καταρτισμον.
7. Along with apostles, prophets, and evangelists (Eph. 4:11).
8. Greek επιχορηγιασ, literally "supply."

ment in a young man like Timothy (Acts 16:3). Years later, he stated to the Philippian church that he hoped to send Timothy to them, a man like no other, that he knew would genuinely be concerned for their welfare (Phil. 2:19–20).

Timothy's work is needed today. The church is in need of men and women who have been equipped to do the work of the ministry and are able and willing to connect with others to do the same (Eph. 4:16). But first, we must ask, "Where are the leaders who will get this process started, and what does it take to be this kind of leader?" This is the subject of the next chapter.

CHAPTER 3

TAKE ME TO YOUR LEADERS

The greatest leader is not necessarily the one
who does the greatest things. He is the one that gets
the people to do the greatest things.

—Ronald Reagan

Great leaders create more leaders, not followers.

—Roy T. Bennett, *The Light in the Heart*

When it comes to the church, there are few topics more important than the subject of leadership. Questions abound like "What is a leader?" or "How do you develop leaders?" When it comes to what the Bible says about leadership, especially leadership in the church, it couldn't be more confusing. Why is it that views about leadership and leadership structures vary so much in the church of today? Have we misunderstood the teaching of the Bible on leadership? Or, and much more concerning, have we seen the teaching of the Bible on leadership and settled for something else?

Sometimes, a person is taken captive by a system of thinking already in place. As a person growing up in the church, I was not fully aware of how the church worked in terms of making decisions. As a pastor, I simply inherited the practice that was already in place and never questioned whether it was the way the church should be led. Now, years later, I believe that was a mistake on my part. My tradition taught us that the church is to be led by a board of people elected through a democratic process. In essence, if a vote was taken and it passed, it must be God's will. Only a careless reading of the Bible will lead one to take such a view.

THE SCOPE OF ROLE CONFUSION

We are living in a strange world where opinions matter more than facts. No one should be offended, and everyone should get the chance to cast their vote or opinion into the pot in order for a decision to be made. What pastor has not been told: "Well, I would run that idea by so-and-so before moving forward." I have often talked with pastors who say that they are dreading discussing a matter with the board that they believe is directly from God. One pastor told me that his board regularly reminds him that *he's not in charge*!

Much, if not all, of this confusion has taken place due to a misunderstanding of the biblical roles for church leadership as they are defined in the Scriptures. People forced into roles for which they were never intended, and the absence of key roles can only lead to confusion and serve as a block to the church ever being able to function as it was intended. One must ask: Can a church that misunderstands and misuses the key roles assigned to it ever expect to function as God intended?

Nowhere does the confusion become more apparent than with those who are charged to lead the church: *elders and deacons.* In addition to those given to the church to *equip the saints* (Eph. 4:11–16), these servant leaders are given *to lead and serve the church* as it pursues God's plan for their ministry. In most churches, those who do not aspire to serve as an elder or deacon on the board often dominate and have a commanding influence or control over what happens in the church. This is very true when clerks, trustees, treasurers, and others are not necessarily spiritually minded. Add to this dysfunction a church body that expects the pastor to preach, visit, and leave the leading of the church to them.

DETAILS MATTER

A closer look at the New Testament's description of the role of elder and deacon can provide an amazing amount of insight into a biblical view of church leadership. 1 Timothy is not necessarily considered a manual of church operations; however, in this letter, the appointment of elders and deacons appears to be necessary, thus the reason for Paul having Timothy remain in Ephesus to oversee the church in his absence (1 Tim. 1:3) and to provide leadership that will be able to deal with false teachers and their teaching (1 Tim. 1:1–7).

Paul's remarks concerning elders and deacons fall under the special category of a "trustworthy saying" (1 Tim. 3:1). The Pastoral Epistles contain five such sayings.[9] The fact that one's aspiration to be an elder is included argues for its significance to the church. In the Greek language, it is rendered πιστοσ ο Λογοσ, meaning "the saying is faithful or trustworthy" This was something that the Ephesian believers could believe and understand in terms of its importance for the role of elder επισκοποσ (elder) in the life of the church. Aspiring to be an elder was not without qualifications. The elder must not be a recent convert, and he must be one in whom godly character traits dwell.[10]

In 1 Timothy 5:17, Paul gives us our first distinction among *elders*. Here Paul used the term πρεσβυτεροι (elders) to identify the elders as those who administrate or rule the life of the church. This particular word may imply that they are older since this is the same term (πρεσβυτεροσ) used to describe the older brother in the gospel story of the prodigal son (Luke 15:25). They are to receive "double honor," especially if they give themselves to preaching and teaching (1 Tim. 5:17). Here, we see that some elders are expected to be able to administrate the life of the church while some are gifted

---

[9.] See also 1 Timothy 1:15, 1 Timothy 3:1, 2 Timothy 2:11, Titus 1:13, and Titus 3:8.
[10.] The elders qualifications included being above reproach, husband of one wife, sober-minded, self-controlled, respectable, hospitable, able to teach, not a drunkard, not violent but gentle, not quarrelsome, not a lover of money, able to manage his own home with dignity, and well-thought-of by outsiders.

to do preaching/teaching and administrate the church. These gifts are seen in full force through Paul's words to Titus when he left him in Crete to "put what remained in order and appoint elders in every town" (Titus 1:5).

WHERE HAVE ALL THE ELDERS GONE?

There is purpose and power behind God's design to place elders and deacons in each church. The trouble is that many churches have only *deacons*, and in a lot of cases, they are expected to act like elders. Taking this approach to church leadership can only lead to confusion for the church as it seeks to identify and develop leaders. The disciples faced this dilemma as the church began to grow (Acts 6:1–7).

As the church began to grow exponentially, some were being neglected in the distribution of food. Wisely, the disciples came together and decided that they could not give up their commitment to preaching the Word in order to serve tables (diakonein), not because they couldn't serve tables but because they had been given a specific calling on their lives and to neglect that would be detrimental to the health and growth of the church.

The Bible's teaching on the ministry of deacons is like that of elders. They must be people that can be trusted with the faith, clean and honest in terms of their character and tested.[11] Since this is such an important ministry role in the life of the church, they should be tested first and only then established as deacons.[12] Through their service, they can gain good standing for themselves and great confidence in their faith. According to Paul and the earlier apostles, this combination of leadership was critical to the ongoing health of the church. Without this type of leadership base, it seems likely that the church would not move forward as a unified whole.

Ideally, the church should be led by elders and deacons who are committed to seeking and following God's plan for the church. It is through this partnership that the church gains confidence about the

---

[11.] See 1 Timothy 3:8–12.
[12.] See 1 Timothy 3:13.

direction of the church and are willing to follow. It is not surprising then that this became the practice of Paul when planting a new church. He knew that the future life of the church depended on it.

THE TIMOTHY FACTOR

Since we now know that Paul gave Timothy instructions on the type of leaders to be established in the church, one must ask why he would give this charge to his young apostolic delegate and send him into a difficult place like Ephesus. We know that one of the reasons that he asked Timothy to join him in his ministry to the churches (Acts 16:1–5) was due to the fact that he recognized in him qualities and characteristics essential for leadership even though he was young and raised in a spiritually divided home (Acts 16:1). The letters to Timothy serve as a great example of what a true leader of the church should look like. A consideration of these qualities requires a deeper look at Timothy's life and ministry in Ephesus so we can discern the real DNA of a biblical leader for the church. We now turn our attention to this matter.

CHAPTER 4

THE TIMOTHY FACTOR

The challenge of leadership is to be strong,
but not rude; be kind, but not weak; be bold, but not a bully;
be thoughtful, but not lazy; be humble, but not timid;
be proud, but not arrogant; have humor, but without folly.

—Jim Rohn

To be a leader in the church, one has to be *smart, well-educated, raised in a Christian home, handsome, have experience in life, and older.* Or do you? This certainly doesn't describe Timothy, Paul's young apostolic delegate that we read about throughout the New Testament.

These two men first met in Lystra, probably on Paul's first missionary journey, then reconnected upon his return visit to Timothy's hometown. It seems reasonable to assume that during Paul's absence, Timothy had matured, and that much of this was due to the influence of his godly grandmother (Lois) and his mother (Eunice).[13] His father was a Greek and a pagan. So coming from a spiritually divided home makes the fact that he was well-thought-of by the brothers at Lystra and Iconium—even more impressive.

[13.] 2 Timothy 1:5.

To be thought of in a favorable light is one thing, but to take off with Paul throughout the known world at that time must have raised some eyebrows. Loved and appreciated by many, no doubt some wondered what in the world Timothy was doing. Nevertheless, Paul, Silas, Timothy, and most importantly, the Holy Spirit, believed this was the right thing to do.

Looking back on their story, one can see that God was up to doing an amazing thing through the relationship that started on that day that would set the stage for the growth of the church and provide for each of us a model of what a true leader looks and acts like. While he had been asked to represent the ministry of Paul in other churches (Phil. 2:19–30; 1 Thess. 2:17–3:5), Timothy's most challenging test came when he was asked to stay in Ephesus (1 Tim. 1:3–5) a number of years later in order to deal with false teachers and lead the church toward "biblical health."[14] I can only imagine what was going through Timothy's mind as he heard this request and remembered his tearful (2 Tim. 1:3–4) departure from Paul as he contemplated being on his own. While Timothy was not technically a pastor as we picture that in our mind, he certainly dealt with similar issues similar to those that we see in the church of today.

WISE WORDS

Timothy was left in Ephesus, but he was not abandoned to be on his own. The letter in 2 Timothy (Paul's final communication to his young apostolic delegate) was filled with words of wisdom—not only for him but for every person charged with establishing and leading a church. To some degree, Timothy's future was uncertain; however, Paul was committed to the belief that he would be fine should he heed the words in his letter (and, more importantly, the things that he had learned throughout his life).

> But as for you, continue in what you have learned
> and have firmly believed, knowing from whom

[14.] 1 Timothy 1:3–4.

you learned it, and how from childhood you have
been acquainted with the sacred writings, which
are able to make you wise for salvation through
faith in Jesus Christ. All Scripture is breathed out
by God and profitable for teaching, for reproof,
for correction, and for training in righteousness
that the man of God may be complete, equipped
for every good work (2 Tim. 3:14–17).

The final words of Paul to Timothy were a challenge to take his
stand against the people who would not endure sound teaching, who
accumulate for themselves teachers to suit their own desires, who
would turn away from truth in order to believe in myths (2 Tim.
4:3–4). According to Paul, the antidote to this ecclesiastical cancer
was quite simple: "As for you, always be sober-minded, endure suffering, do the work of an evangelist, [and] fulfill your ministry" (2
Tim. 4:5).

What the apostle meant by these final words is to be seen as
a summary of the whole. He is to be *sober-minded*, that is, not a
drunkard (1 Tim. 3:3). More likely, this is an admonition to be *clear-
minded* in terms of what is right or wrong. Do not allow yourself
to be negatively impacted by those who oppose your message or do
you harm (2 Tim. 4:14–15). He is to *endure suffering*, not only in a
passive sense of encountering difficulty but also in an active sense
that might include suffering evil at the hands of evildoers. As an
evangelist, he was *to do the work of an evangelist*, which meant not
only preaching the Word but being ready to do so through every
relationship (regardless how toxic it may be). Finally, he was to *fulfill
his ministry*.[15]

---

15. Πληροθορησον, meaning "complete," or "do one's absolute utmost or everything conceivably possible."

WHAT ABOUT TODAY?

Living by these standards would change everything for today's pastor of a church. Imagine what the contemporary church might look like with a clear-minded leader who would hang in there despite any trouble he might face, one who would continue to share the gospel no matter what his opposition might be, and who would be absolutely committed to doing the work of his ministry according to the biblical standard given by Paul to Timothy.

While *compromise* is not necessarily a bad word, it is unacceptable in the life of the believer and the church when it means the amalgamation of our most significant convictions with the way of the world. We are to be pure (1 Tim. 1:5), truthful (Eph. 4:15), sincere (2 Tim. 1:5), and obedient (2 Tim. 4:1–5, 1 Pet. 1:14). To suggest that we are and do otherwise will never fulfill God's plan for the church.

THE TIMOTHY FACTOR

What then does it look like to become a godly person, one in whom people can trust and follow as they lead a ministry? What are the identifiable and distinguishing traits of a leader and (especially a pastor) who seeks to be used mightily for the advancement of the church?

Over the years of their partnership, Timothy had heard and seen many things and even been challenged to remember and practice these truths, some of which he had learned as a child (2 Tim. 3:14–16). Perhaps nothing summarizes Paul's intent better than these words:

> Follow the pattern of the sound words that you have heard from me in the faith and love that are in Christ Jesus. By the Holy Spirit who dwells within us guard the good deposit entrusted to you. (2 Tim. 1:13–14)

> Do your best to present yourself to God as one approved, a worker who has no need to be ashamed, rightly handling the word of truth. (2 Tim. 2:15)

After a careful reading and study of Paul's final letter to Timothy (2 Tim.), one can hardly miss the obvious and intentional embedding of these godly characteristics in Paul's parting advice to his young and faithful apostolic delegate. In the remainder of this chapter, I want to describe what has become known to me as the *Timothy factor*.[16] Through obedience to these five traits (although they are not an exhaustive list), Timothy would be able to fulfill his ministry in Ephesus in the spirit spoken of by Peter the Elder.[17]

> Shepherd the flock of God that is among you, exercising oversight, not under compulsion, but willingly, as God would have you, not for shameful gain, but eagerly, not domineering over those in your charge, but being examples to the flock. (1 Pet. 5:2–3)

UNHYPOCRITICAL FAITH (2 TIMOTHY 1:3–7)

Did something happen to remind Paul of Timothy and their tearful departure? Why was he constantly on his mind and in his prayers? Was it nothing more than the fact that he loved his companion and longed to see him knowing that it would be a joyful reunion? Perhaps it was because he knew Timothy's mother (Eunice) and his grandmother (Lois), who no doubt was the major reason that Timothy was a man of faith.

---

16. The **Timothy factor** is described as the impact made by Timothy in the ministry at Ephesus through the life of Timothy as he adhered to five traits of a godly leader.
17. 1 Peter 5:2–3.

Many leaders can attest to the influence of their parents. This must have been true for Timothy, given the fact that he was raised in a family that was split along religious lines. While his mom was a proselyte from Judaism to Christianity, his dad was a nonbeliever. The fact that Timothy's spiritual maturity caught the attention of Paul to the point that he wanted him to accompany him on his upcoming mission trips is quite amazing.

There is no question that he was a fine young man, a person of good character and one in whom there was significant evidence of faith. The attraction of Timothy to Paul was not due to his looks, his training, or his experience. No, there was something quite impressive about this young man that was only beginning to blossom, and it was enough for Paul to know that he wanted him to join their team. By the time Paul wrote to Timothy when he lived in Ephesus, this young man had grown into a man of faith and one worthy of trust.

The remembrance that was lodged in Paul's mind was the *sincere* or *genuine* nature of his young apostolic delegate's faith. It was a quality of faith that he first observed in his mother and grandmother. Now, years later, there was no doubt that this same faith dwelt in Timothy—a faith that he would need as he dealt with the false teachers in Ephesus. The goal of Timothy's ministry in Ephesus was love that came from *a pure heart, a good conscience, and a sincere faith* (1 Tim. 1:5), an arsenal that would be needed on a daily basis. The first two are built on the last, which is best described by Paul through the use of the word *sincere*, describing the *unhypocritical nature* of his faith.[18] Young Timothy was not a pretender or one known to wear a mask as an actor would use to act like a character in a play. He would never pretend to care for someone or something or present himself to be someone that he in reality is not.

The story is told that Daniel Day-Lewis, while acting in the movie as Abraham Lincoln, would remain in character even during the breaks taken during the shooting of the movie. Like Lewis, leaders need to be the same regardless of their setting. Serving as a pastor

---

18. Ανυποκριτου, a term used to describe the nature of hypocrisy.

of the church demands the same kind of tenacity when it comes to saying one thing and doing another. Apparently, this is a real issue for Christians. In the year 2009, David Kinnaman and Gabe Lyons discovered through an extensive survey of non-Christians that the two things most thought of about the behavior of Christians were *hypocrisy* and *judgmentalism.*[19]

TODAY'S CHALLENGE

What then is the antidote for a church in need of leadership? It certainly is not a program or a flashy and charismatic person who can simply attract a crowd. No, the church of today needs and hungers for today's leaders that live by the same principles and traits found in Timothy. Indeed, Timothy was both a young and shy man; yet he possessed at least one character trait that made all the difference. He was a man of integrity, one who could be trusted to carry out the work he had been commissioned to do. He was a man with an *unhypocritical faith*—a person who could be given the responsibility of leading a ministry in the fulfillment of Christ's mandate for the church.[20]

The reality for today's church is the task of searching and finding men like Timothy in whom the privilege of leading the church can be given.

UNQUESTIONABLE PURPOSE
(2 TIMOTHY 1:8–9)

It doesn't take long for a leader to realize that being a nice person will not get them to their intended goal. They must have a *purpose* that gives meaning to what they are trying to do—one that is worthy of the effort being made. One might expect the Apostle Paul

---

[19.] David Kinnaman and Gabe Lyons, *unChristian: What a New Generation Really Thinks about Christianity…and Why It Matters* (Baker Book Publishing Company, 2007).

[20.] Matthew 28:16–20.

to throw in the towel after beatings, imprisonments, rejections, and abuse; but even after all of this, he was more determined to press on. You can hear it in his words:

> I thank him who has given me strength, Christ Jesus our Lord, because he judged me faithful, appointing me to his service, though formerly I was a blasphemer, persecutor, and insolent opponent. But I received mercy because I had acted ignorantly in unbelief, and the grace of our Lord overflowed for me with the faith and love that are in Christ Jesus. The saying is trustworthy and deserving of full acceptance that Christ Jesus came into the world to save sinners of whom I am the foremost. **But I received mercy for this reason, that in me, as the foremost, Jesus Christ might display his perfect patience as an example to those who were to believe in him for eternal life.** To the King of the ages, immortal, invisible, the only God, be honor and glory forever and ever. Amen. (1 Tim. 1:12–17)

Leaders in the church must know why they are given the chance to display the same love of Christ to those that they lead. Like Timothy, who received this same charge from Paul,[21] we, as leaders of today's church, understand this privilege to be given to us solely based on the work of Christ, "who saved us and called us to a holy calling, not because of our works but because of his own purpose and grace, which he gave us in Christ Jesus before the ages began, and which now has been manifested through the appearing of our Savior Christ Jesus, who abolished death and brought life and immortality to light through the gospel" (2 Tim. 1:9–10).

[21.] 1 Timothy 1:18.

My experience working with churches has shown me that the lack of a clear sense of purpose for the church is not uncommon. Could it be that this exists due to the fact that those who are charged with leading the church are confused as well? Timothy was told "not to be ashamed of the testimony about our Lord, nor of me [Paul] his prisoner, but share in the suffering for the gospel by the power of God" (2 Tim. 1:8). Few people are willing to suffer for something that they don't believe in, but many have suffered and died because they did believe.

The godly leader knows what Christ has done for him and is willing to share that with others regardless of what it brings their way. The leader cannot do this on their own, but through the power and presence of the Holy Spirit, they can make every effort to be faithful in this area of their ministry. Armed with a sincere faith and a clear purpose, the godly leader can now forge forward into whatever ministry he is led to assume.

> Follow the pattern of the sound words that you have heard from me in the faith and love that are in Christ Jesus. By the Holy Spirit who dwells within us, guard the good deposit entrusted to you. (2 Tim. 1:13–14)

UNCOMPROMISING PROCESS
(2 TIMOTHY 2:1–7)

Having godly character and a clear understanding of the purpose of your life and ministry can never guarantee its success. Those who lead a church must also have a strategy designed to achieve its ultimate goal and a way to implement their chosen plan of action. Paul's words to Timothy reveal a simple plan for making this happen:

> You then, my child, be strengthened by the grace that is in Christ Jesus, and what you have heard from me in the presence of many **witnesses**

entrust to faithful men who will be able to teach others also. (2 Tim. 2:1–2)

At the heart of Paul's words to Timothy, we find what Jim Putman calls *real-life discipleship.*[22] When it comes to discipleship, says Putman, "*relationships* are the pipeline that deliver the precious ingredients of discipleship and make disciple-making possible."[23] One might wonder why Jesus spent three and one-half years with his disciples. Mark records that when He appointed the twelve disciples, He did so that they might be **with** Him (Mark 3:14). Jesus was with His disciples because His relationship with them was the pipeline through which He would give them all that they needed. He did it this way because He knew that *more is caught than taught.*

Billy Graham, who is perhaps the greatest evangelist to ever live and preach, was once asked what he would do differently should he start his ministry over again. Graham's response was quite surprising given the fact that he had preached all over the world and seen more people than anyone respond to the gospel in faith. Graham answered the question in this way: "If I had to start all over again, I would pick twelve men, spend time with them investing my life into theirs, and trust God to use them to touch the world."[24]

It is exactly the same as the advice given to Timothy by Paul when he told him to *entrust* all that he had learned to faithful men who would pass it on to others (2 Tim. 2:2). Through the relationships that Timothy would have with *faithful men,* the ministry of Paul and the teaching that he proclaimed would continue on as they did the same with others. This would not be easy at all, and it would include suffering, but as he abode by the rules given by Paul, he

---

[22] Jim Putnam, Real Life Discipleship *Building Churches that make disciples* (NavPress, P.O. Box 35001, Colorado, CO 80935, 2010), pg. 21

[23] Kinnaman and Lyons, *unChristian*, pg. 47.

[24] This response was heard by me listening to an interview of Billy Graham on a TV talk show while in seminary.

would be blessed with the fruit of changed lives—people who would be committed to the Christ and eager to do the same.[25]

How many pastors/preachers will regret the fact that they took a different approach to building disciples? They will at least learn what didn't work. Programs, extended large group teaching sessions, small groups that read a book about making disciples and never seek to apply the principles they have learned, and more will come up short on carrying out Christ's mandate to make disciples (Matt. 28:16–20).

According to Ron Bennet in his book *Intentional Disciplemaking: Cultivating Spiritual Maturity in the Local Church*, disciple-making is to be done at the individual level:

> There are many areas in the family of God that allow for blending and being interdependent, but discipleship is not one of them. We can learn in groups, we can serve in teams, we can worship as a family, but we can only be disciples individually. A ministry that seeks to make disciples must support the personal responsibility and accountability required in developing individual discipleship. It can use a variety of methods, but it must always bring discipleship to the personal level of each individual.[26]

Bennett suggests that it's not the knowing but the holding of truth that marks someone as a disciple of Christ. Too often, Christians are *knowledge rich but application poor.* We pride ourselves in having the *right* doctrine, but without conviction—the kind that leads to

---

[25.] In 2 Timothy 2:3–7, here Paul encourages Timothy to continue to do this despite the possibility of suffering from the hands of those who oppose him. He must keep faithful to the "rules" given by Paul and take time to think carefully about what he is doing and the fruit that is coming from his efforts.

[26.] Ron Bennett, *Intentional Disciplemaking: Cultivating Spiritual Maturity in the Local Church* (NavPress, PO Box 6000, Colorado Springs, CO 80934), pg. 15.

commitment, competence, and *character development*—our lifestyles differ little from the cultural norm and don't even hint at Christ within us.[27]

The pastor who wants to effectively lead his church toward biblical heath must possess an unhypocritical faith, a clear purpose, and an uncompromising commitment to a process of relational and personal disciple-making. But what's next?

UNRELENTLESS COMMITMENT (2 TIMOTHY 2:8–13)

I can remember clearly the early days of my first pastorate. Like any pastor, I wanted to do the very best that I could do in proclaiming the teaching of the Bible. On one occasion, I made the decision to preach on a passage of Scripture found in 2 Timothy 2:8–10, where Paul speaks of being chained like a criminal.

The only way I could think of getting into the real sense of this text was to experience the "being chained like a criminal" part. At the time, I lived in New England, where most of the houses have basements. The one that we lived in not only had a basement, it had a creepy, dirty, and somewhat scary basement. It had beams that served as support for the house and a whole lot of clutter that had been stored down there for years. In all honesty, it was more like a dungeon than a basement. Nevertheless, I thought that it would serve as a perfect site for a prison experience.

You can imagine the reaction of my young bride when I told her my idea. "You're going to do what?" So off I went into the dark confines of *my* prison. I even had my wife chain me to a pole and bring me bread and water every couple of hours. I can't remember how long I stayed down there, but it was most of the day. What I do remember is how I felt and some of the things that went through my mind. Being on your back in the dirt and darkness in a place crawling with bugs has a way of making you think about a lot of things.

[27.] Ibid., pg. 19.

You may laugh at my experiment, but it was quite revealing to me. I discovered some important things about myself and about the apostle Paul. I can understand why Paul might reach the point where he was more concerned about the gospel and its integrity than his well-being. At some point, it would become easy to resign yourself at some point to never getting out of prison. Paul had accepted the possibility that this might be the end of his life, and he was willing to accept that reality. No one would argue that Paul was not in a difficult position in prison, and that perhaps he was thinking that this would be the end of his life and ministry. It is not surprising to hear him talk about being torn between two possibilities: remaining in the body or departing and being with Christ (Phil. 1:23).

I realize that my attempt to understand some of the emotional and physical trauma that almost certainly was part of Paul's experience falls way short of what he actually went through. Interestingly, I discovered that nothing I went through that day was something that I could endure for a long time. In just a few hours, I was ready to leave. I am quite certain my thoughts would have been even more intense had I not known that I could leave.

The most amazing part of this testimony of Paul is the fact that he didn't seem to be bothered even though he knew that he wasn't a criminal, and yet he was chained as if he were one. I don't know about you, Pastor, but I most likely would have been demanding that I be let go. Even though he was suffering and being bound by chains, he was able to look on the brighter side of his situation for one reason: he was totally convinced of the gospel of Jesus Christ. He was okay with being in prison because of trumped up charges so that others might be set free (2 Tim. 10).

This was not the first time that Paul had had the chance to speak about what happens in or out of his prison cell (Phil. 1:12–18). You might think that he would be overly concerned about things that he can't control but he wasn't. In his letter to the Philippian Christians, he makes his view perfectly clear:

> I want you to know, brothers, that what has
> happened to me has really served to advance the

gospel, so that it has become known throughout the whole imperial guard and to all the rest that my imprisonment is for Christ. And most of the brothers, having become confident in the Lord by my imprisonment, are much bolder to speak the work without fear.

Some indeed preach Christ from envy and rivalry, but others from good will. The latter do it out of love, knowing that I am put here for the defense of the gospel. The former proclaims Christ out of selfish ambition, not sincerely but thinking to afflict me in my imprisonment. What then? Only that in every way, whether in pretense or in truth, Christ is proclaimed, and in that I rejoice.[28]

Paul's response to his plight was a statement of *unrelentless commitment* to do whatever was necessary to bring glory to Christ Jesus. He knew that this is what the Lord demanded for those who follow Him. Rather than complaining, Paul was content to stay put in prison even while the message of the gospel was advancing, and he couldn't be involved. To do otherwise would be in conflict with the expectation of Christ.

If we have died with him, we will also live with him;
If we endure, we will also reign with him;
If we deny him, he also will deny us,
If we are faithless, he remains faithful for he cannot deny himself. (2 Tim. 2:11)

Any church would love to find a leader who demonstrates an *unhypocritical faith, is driven by a clear sense of purpose for the church,*

---

28. Philippians 1:12–18.

possesses an understanding of how to make disciples, and be committed to fulfil the missional mandate given by Christ regardless of what he had to endure. As Timothy came to the end of this final letter from his mentor, one question must have been ever on his mind: "How do I do this?" The answer is coming, so please, read on.

UNENDING OBEDIENCE (2 TIMOTHY 4:1–8)

Preaching has always been at the center of what a pastor does in the life of a church, so it is not surprising that the emphasis upon preaching is at the heart of Paul's final charge given to Timothy. He gave it against the background of the promised appearing of Jesus, who will judge the living and the dead (2 Tim. 4:1). It stands to reason that if *preaching* is your primary responsibility in the church, you should be faithful to this task in the fullest sense.

Throughout my time at Bible college and seminary, I was taught how to study the Bible in its original setting so that I would be able to apply it to my present life situation. This meant understanding a host of things that contribute to an accurate understanding such as *genre, context,* and *content* questions.[29] Throw in a class here and there on *homiletics*[30] and I was ready to preach—or was I?

Given the situation in Ephesus, it is more likely than not that Paul was thinking about much more than the act of preaching as we know it. He was not thinking about Timothy standing in front of the believers in Ephesus, expounding on the gospel and Old Testament truths. Besides remembering Paul's teaching about the gospel message, where was he to get his material? It appears that he had been in training for years.

[29.] *Genre* is a category of composition such as wisdom, gospel, historical narrative, and apocalyptic. *Context* refers to the circumstances that form the setting for an event, statement, or idea and in terms of which it can be fully understood and assessed. *Content* refers the meanings of words and concepts as defined by the context and culture.

[30.] *Homiletics* refers to the art of preaching or writing sermons.

> But as for you, continue in what have learned and have firmly believed, knowing from whom you have learned it and how from childhood you have been acquainted with the sacred writings which are able to make you wise for salvation through faith in Christ Jesus. (2 Tim. 3:141–15)

Conservative estimates suggest that Timothy was somewhere between thirty to thirty-five years old at this point in his life, which implies that he had enough exposure to the truth lived out in Paul's life to make a difference (or at least, Paul thought so). This confidence in Paul came from his understanding of the power of Scripture to change lives.

> All Scripture is breathed out by God and profitable for teaching, for reproof, for correction, and for training in righteousness, that the man of God may be complete, equipped for every good work. (2 Tim. 3:16–17)

The fact that the Scriptures were "God-breathed" (2 Tim. 3:16) made all the difference for Paul as he delivered these final words of advice (2 Tim. 3:10–17). It was by adhering to these words of guidance that Timothy would become "complete, equipped for every good work."[31] Through the Scriptures, Timothy would have an understanding of God's plan of salvation (2 Tim. 3:15), doctrine, and truth to support him in his ministry (2 Tim. 3:16) and a warning to protect himself and every believer from meandering away from God's will for their lives (2 Tim. 3:17).

[31.] The use of the perfect tense here suggest that this is an abiding condition provided he allow the Scripture to do its work of bringing his pursuit of maturity to an end.

WHAT ABOUT TODAY'S PASTOR?

All of a sudden, we realize that the charge to "preach the Word" means more than we ever thought it meant. To *preach the Word* means to be fully engaged in the work of taking the truths of the Scripture to the streets. A lot of hard work has already taken place, but now we must put feet to our message. Understanding what a text meant in its original setting is only the beginning of what a preacher is expected to do. Does it include when we walk off the platform after preaching a message and someone challenges our thoughts, when we are confronted in a meeting with what we are saying or planning on doing, when we are on the ball field and we notice a behavior unbecoming of a believer, and even when we experience opposition from someone in the community about what we represent? YES, this is preaching the Word.

I CAN ONLY IMAGINE

Very few people are unfamiliar with the song written by the lead singer of MercyMe, Bart Millard. He wrote the song as a response to his father's death, which caused him to contemplate what it would be like to be in the presence of God. For a moment, allow me to ask you to imagine something else. As we consider the present-day condition of the church and the many issues it faces, are we willing to ask that very important question: *What if?* What if we took seriously the charge given to Timothy regarding the church? What if we, as pastors and leaders of the church, make these a priority? What if we pursued an unhypocritical faith, a passionate attempt to share the gospel message in all that we do and wherever we go? What if we diligently seek to pass on our faith to faithful men and women who will do the same? And what if we preach and live out the Word in every situation we encounter? *What if? I can only imagine!*

With Paul giving so much attention to the priority and importance of preaching the Word, it seems appropriate that we now look at how one reaches the point when they know what God's Word is telling us to do. If you are willing to dig deep, let's go!

CHAPTER 5

PREACH THE WORD

You can read the bible, and should,
but until you study it, it doesn't come alive for
you and teach you a lasting lesson.

—Gail Davis

It's Sunday morning, and you've been asked to preach at your local church. You're nervous and if you weren't, I'd have concerns that you were approaching this responsibility in your own strength and wisdom. The most important question as you approach this task is a little different than the typical question of "what are you preaching about?" It is important that one preach from a Bible text that addresses the topic, yet there is so much more to this task.

I do not want to suggest that understanding the text is not important. Every preacher must first have a clear grasp of the passage's meaning on so many levels. That is to say, he must know what is going on in the culture when this message was communicated (context), and his work is only beginning because now he must seek to understand what type of *genre* he is reading. Perhaps he is using wisdom or poetry literature. It could be that the text is embedded in the middle of *historical narrative*. It is possible that his message is coming out of the *Gospels* or the *Epistles* written in the New Testament. It really gets exciting when the pastor chooses to preach from a passage found in the *apocalyptic* parts of the Bible such as Daniel or Revelation, where he must understand what a dragon represents. Speaking of being nervous, preaching from one of these texts just might heighten my anxiety as I walk toward the platform to preach. The message could be coming from a sermon, parable, or riddle which is found in a larger type of literature. That's one reason I have been helped tremendously through the years by the work of Douglas Stuart and Gordon Fee in their insightful work entitled *How to Read the Bible for All It's Worth.*[32] Preaching from a text in these contexts demand that we have a clear understanding of how to interpret the material.

Knowing the type of literature (genre) you are preaching from and the boundaries of the text puts the preacher in a position where he can now discover the meaning of the words (content) used to convey the message of the author. This is true because words only have meaning in a given context. Knowing what the words mean and how they are used in the original context will shed light on what is really being said and how it is to be understood. Once this is in place, a preacher can factor in an accurate understanding of his own culture and make a decision about what this means today. Can you imagine forsaking this process today and demanding from the pulpit that we must greet one another with a *holy kiss or literally forsake your mother and father?*

Perhaps one of the most difficult and challenging pieces of this process is to determine the primary point of a given text. Again, relying on the work of Stuart and Fee, a text can only have one main point. It can have a variety of applications but only one point. This is also one of the reasons that some of the preaching coming out of our pulpits are so dangerous. One must consider, can or will the Holy Spirit, who is the one who applies the teachings of the Scripture (Eph. 6:17), use a sermon effectively if the interpretation of the Scripture is wrong?

One of the basic rules of biblical hermeneutics that I learned many years ago goes like this: let Scripture interpret Scripture. This

---

[32.] Gordon D. Fee and Douglas Stuart, *How to Read the Bible for All it's Worth* (Zondervan, 3900 Sparks Drive Street, Grand Rapids, MI 49546, 2014).

really helps when one is trying to wrap their mind around the writings of the Apostle Paul, given the fact that he wrote twelve of the twenty-seven books of the New Testament. A preacher certainly must check all of the passages dealing with the same subject that Paul has written in order to understand his position on a particular topic (e.g., role of women in the church, etc.). Add to this rule of interpretation the idea of *historical distance*. What is true for the first century may be accurate for both the culture of the text, as well as the culture of the hearers (i.e., first century) but applied differently.

Preachers who neglect these exegetical guidelines are likely to end up preaching something that is far from the truth and the intended meaning of the text. What then is the most appropriate way of preaching the Word of God today? I know that many people would answer that question in this way: "I like the way our pastor preaches because he's funny, and I can understand him," or "I don't see anything wrong with the way our pastor preaches. His messages make me feel good!" While these are positive traits and can be useful, they are not the *litmus test* for what constitutes a great message. If this is so, what is the most appropriate way to prepare and preach a great sermon for delivery to the church body today?

WORKING HARD OR HARDLY WORKING?

A simple formula for preaching a biblical and acceptable sermon can be boiled down to three basic steps: (1) Determine the context; that is, what was it like at the time of the writing? (2) Understand the content[33] in light of the particular context and culture surrounding the text, and (3) take the meaning of the text in its original context, and apply it to the cultural context of the person reading the passage.

As previously mentioned, since "a holy kiss" (Rom. 16:16) was understood and practiced in the first century in a certain way and for a specific reason, are we to practice it in an identical manner today in

---

[33] *Content* concerns itself with the question of meaning. In this case, what does a word mean in the original context, and why should it be understood in this way?

the twenty-first century? If not, why not, and how should we practice the original intent of a holy kiss in the culture of those receiving the letter that will honor its original purpose and practice?

DETAILS *DO* MATTER

It may be that many pastors bypass or neglect the hard work of exegesis because they are what my dad used to call concordance preachers. This is a preacher who works hard looking up Scripture references on a given subject and never giving attention to whether or not each appearance of the word is the same word and carries with it the same meaning or whether or not the context of a word is giving the word an alternate interpretation of meaning. As an example, let's take the word *love* and look at how a preacher might have a problem following this pattern of biblical study prior to preparing and preaching a sermon.

I would never take the position that a pastor who has never had training in the *exegesis*[34] of the Bible shouldn't be in the role of preacher. I would, however, say that a preacher who is equipped to understand a particular word used in a text is in a better position to "preach the Word." It will be very important to know whether the word *phileo* (φιλεω) or *agape* (αγαπη) is being used by the author in order for the preacher to understand and present the meaning of a text. It is clear from the discourse between Jesus and Peter in John 21:15–19 that Jesus knew the difference between these words as He advised Peter how He wanted him to serve Him. One would notice in this passage that Jesus begins by calling Peter to the higher level of agape love but moved toward Peter by using his word for love (φιλεω), indicating Peter's humility in not being able to love at the level Jesus was asking for.

A similar situation occurs when reading a New Testament passage on the subject of *hell*. One must know which word is being used *Hades* (αδη), *Gehenna* (γεννα), *or Tartarus* (ταρταροσ)in the text.

---

34. The term *exegesis* means "to draw or pull out the original meaning of a text."

A proper interpretation is dependent on which word the author uses. How does one interpret a passage like Luke 16:19–31, where Jesus tells a story about a man being in *hades* (verse 23)? Is the man in the grave (Hades), which is a place or abode of the dead, similar to the Old Testament word *Sheol*.[35] The answer might seem simple but perhaps not.

Jesus spoke many times about judgement, and in every case, He used the word *Gehenna*, not *Hades*. So one might ask, why wouldn't He use it here when the text clearly is speaking about judgment? Many suggest that this is not Jesus's story but one that was familiar in the first century context.

By examining each occurrence of the word, one will discover that the word *hell* can range in meaning from a place of judgment, the grave or abode of the dead, to a mythological place where rebellious gods were confined. The most common word translated *hell* in the New Testament is the word *Gehenna*, which is referred to as the place of judgment.[36] In every case, Jesus speaks of Gehenna with reference to judgment, while *Hades* refer to the grave or place of the dead. In the only other places where different words are used for *hell* (Luke 16:23, *hell*; 2 Peter 2:4, *tartarosas*), one can examine the context and determine that something other than judgment is meant.

The rich man in this story is so desperate that he longs for Lazarus to be permitted to go back to life and tell his family about this place. He argues, "If someone comes back from the dead they will repent" (Luke 16:30). The passage ends with Abraham telling the rich man that there's plenty of truth written in the Books of Moses and the prophets for them to believe, and furthermore, "even if someone should rise from the dead" (Luke 16:31), they will not believe.

Clearly Jesus is speaking to the idea that the Pharisees would rather believe their own stories instead of the truth found in their own Scriptures. Having missed this, it was very unlikely that they

---

[35.] Old Testament word meaning "place of the dead."
[36.] Matthew 5:22, 29; 10:28; 18:9; 23:15, 23:32; Mark 9:43, 45, 47; and Luke 12:5.

would believe in Christ even when He rises from the dead, which is the reason Jesus told their story in the first place.

WHY THIS MATTERS

So what if the words are different? Why does it matter? It matters because words have meaning in context. To treat the Word of God so casually and without depth of interpretation, understanding, and application, the preacher will be led, as well as the people who receive his message, to think something that is not necessarily true about the text.

It is the opinion of this author that this is quite often the end result of what is called *topical preaching*. That is, we pick a topic, find passages of Scripture that seem to speak about the topic at hand (e.g., love or hell), and draw conclusions of our own. And sometimes, those conclusions are wrong and suggest that something is true when it is not. When it is a matter of practice like "greet one another with a holy kiss," we potentially violate a basic principle of interpretation known as the *historical distance* application of a text, which states *a text cannot mean something today that it did not or could not have meant in its original context*. For example, to argue that we should or must practice the "holy kiss" in the twenty-first century as it was done in the first century, we remove the historical distance. To do this would suggest that giving everyone you know a "holy kiss" is acceptable, and that everyone is comfortable with it and knows what and why you are doing it. There may be a place today that might be okay with this practice (e.g., France), but it is safe to say that most would not. However, by understanding the meaning of the "holy kiss" and its significance in its original setting, we are able to find an appropriate gesture for our context that conveys the same meaning (e.g., handshake, hug, high five).

THE ULTIMATE GOAL

The primary goal in preaching messages that promote *sound doctrine* is not to say "I am right" but to know God's Word in order that we might live in a way that pleases Him and be able to pass these truths on to others. The preaching of a biblical text is not an *end* in itself. A preacher does not do all of the work necessary to understand what the Bible says and leave it alone. The initial task is to understand the Word of God, and apply it personally before it is shared with others, especially in the form of a sermon. Paul made this clear in his communication with the Christians in Colossae:

> Let the word of Christ dwell in you richly, teaching and admonishing one another in all wisdom, singing psalms and hymns and spiritual songs, with thankfulness in your hearts to God. (Col. 3:16)

For a believer to be fully equipped for every good work (2 Tim. 3:17), the preacher is charged with preaching the *word* (λογοσ) so it might become the Word (ρηεμα/ρημα) of God. This is the word Jesus used in the wilderness to confront the trickery of Satan: "Man shall not live by bread alone, but by every word that comes from the mouth of God (Matt. 4:4). This is the word of God used by the Spirit of God (Eph. 6:17), and when it is received, it is able to cut to the deepest part of man.

> For the word of God is living and active, sharper than any two-edged sword, piercing to the division of soul and of spirit, of joints and of marrow, and discerning the thoughts and intentions of the heart. (Heb. 4:12)

In his final communication to young Timothy, Paul reminded him of the work he is to carry out against the false teachers in Ephesus:

> Do your best to present yourself to God as one approved, a worker who has no need to be ashamed, rightly dividing the word of truth. (2 Tim. 2:15)

He is to avoid irreverent babble which will lead to more and more ungodliness (2 Tim. 2:16) and pay attention to Scripture which is God-breathed.[37] David, the shepherd king, was also aware of this amazing attribute of God's word.

> The sum of your word is truth, and every one of your righteous rules endures forever. (Ps. 119:160)

Perhaps that is the reason that only two verses in the entire 119th chapter in the Book of Psalms does not mention God's word, rules, law, commandments, or precepts. Like Timothy, David realized that his only hope was to put his trust into the author of the Word of God. Listen carefully to the language of David as he makes this declaration:

> How can a young man keep his way pure? By guarding it according to your word.[38]
> I have stored up your word in my heart that I might not sin against you.[39]
> Give me understanding that I may keep your law and observe it with my whole heart.[40]
> Remember your word to your servant, in which you have made me hope.[41]
> My soul longs for your salvation: I hope in your word.[42]
> I will never forget your precepts, for by them you have given me life. I am yours; save me, for I have sought your precepts.[43]

---

[37] 2 Timothy 3:16–17.
[38] Psalm 119:9.
[39] Psalm 119:11.
[40] Psalm 119:34.
[41] Psalm 119:49.
[42] Psalm 119:81.
[43] Psalm 119:93–94.

Your word is a lamp unto my feet and a light to my path.[44]

You are my hiding place and my shield; I hope in your word.[45]

The sum of your word is truth, and every one of your righteous rules endures forever.[46]

Let my cry come before you, O Lord; give me understanding according to your word.[47]

My tongue will sing of your word, for all your commandments are right.[48]

The ultimate goal of preaching and teaching the Word is *transformation*, first, for the preacher and then for the rest of the church. The truths revealed through the Holy Spirit and written on a page must move to the inner panels of one's heart. At birth, each of us entered a sinful world and are exhorted to reject the thinking and behavior of this world by being "transformed by the renewal of your mind, that by testing you may discern what is the will of God, what is good and acceptable and perfect" (Rom. 12:2).

While the original disciples were not perfect, they *were* changed, especially after experiencing the resurrection of Jesus and the receiving of the Holy Spirit at Pentecost (Acts 2). Filled with the Holy Spirit, the disciples could now set their mind on fulfilling His mandate to make disciples who make disciples (Matt. 28:16–20).

This was the message of the early church which, according to John's writing (1 John 1:1–4), must continue in and through the lives of the people who have been eternally changed by His love and incorporated into his body the church. The ultimate goal is that more and more people will enjoy the fellowship of the church and take up the charge that was given by Christ to His original disciples.

---

44. Psalm 119:105.
45. Psalm 119:114.
46. Psalm 119:160.
47. Psalm 119:169.
48. Psalm 119:172.

That work continues today and must continue until Jesus returns. While preachers have a major role in making this a priority through the preaching of the Word, each of us as believers must let the Word of God dwell richly in our hearts (Col. 3:16) so that whatever we do, whether in word or in deed, it will be done "in the name of the Lord Jesus, giving thanks to God the Father through him."[49]

The message preached from our pulpits today must be a truthful and clear presentation of God's Word discerned through a diligent study and practice, first, by the preacher and then by those who hear it. It is not enough to simply hear the Word; we must be doers of the Word.[50] Notice the words of John the apostle when he speaks of people who hear the message of the Word but never do it.

> This is the message we have heard from him and proclaim to you, that God is light, and in him is no darkness at all. **If we say** we have fellowship with him while we walk in darkness, we lie a do not practice the truth. **But if we walk in the light**, as he is in the light, we have fellowship with one another, and the blood of Jesus his Son cleanses us from all sin. **If we say** we have no sin, we deceive ourselves, and the truth is not in us. **If we confess our sins,** he is faithful and just to forgive us our sins ad to cleanse us from all unrighteousness. **If we say** we have not sinned, we make him a liar, **and his word is not in us.**

There will always be people who hear the preaching of the Word yet never become the kind of people God desires. The call upon the church is to preach the Word so people can understand His Word and put it into practice. This is why we need preachers. But there is more. We need men and women who will live out the message of life in Christ and pass it on to others.

---

[49] Colossians 3:17.
[50] James 1:22–25.

This is called disciple-making (Matt. 28:16–20), and unfortunately very few churches are doing it in the way the Scriptures describe it.

In the next chapter, we will take a careful look at what it means to be a disciple and the process of how you make them (2 Tim. 2:1–2). If you are up for the challenge of what that means, keep reading!

CHAPTER 6

JUST THE FACTS

We have moved so far away from Jesus's command
that many Christians don't have a frame of reference
for what disciple making looks like.

—Francis Chan

I have to admit it, I had never noticed the words of Jesus in John 17:4, which read, "I glorified you on earth, having accomplished the work that you gave me to do." The words are surprising since I had always focused on the primary reasons that Jesus came into this world to die on the cross, be raised from the dead, and ascend back to the Father until He returns in the future to claim His church. While this is true, this writing of Jesus's words by John suggests that Jesus was referring to something else. But what could it be?

These words came during a night of praying to the Father just before He was preparing to leave this life and return to Him (John 17:11). One might wonder what was going through the mind of Jesus as He faced His final hours. After reading John's record of Jesus's prayer, little doubt exists as to what Jesus was thinking. By taking a closer look at His words, we can see that at least three things were most central to His prayer. First, Jesus was certain that He had clearly presented the heart of the gospel, which was to know God and His Son, Jesus Christ (John 17:5). This was the essence of what it meant to have eternal life.

Next, John tells us that Jesus spoke of finishing "the work" that the Father had given him to do, but what was He talking about? One thing's for sure, He was not speaking of His work on the cross or His victory over the grave. He was not talking about His ascension. This prayer was prior to these happening. He had something different on His mind. After reading Jesus's entire prayer, it seems clear that He was talking about His relationship with His disciples. No doubt, He was reflecting on three years of His time with these men. Mark wrote in 3:14 that Jesus called these men to be "with" Him, and now that was coming to an end.

> And he appointed twelve (whom he also named apostles) so they might be **with him** and he might send them out to preach and have authority to cast out demons. (Mark 3:14)

For these three years, Jesus poured His life into these men, all for the purpose of turning them into (as Pastor Jim Putman would say) "real-life disciples." Jesus had accomplished the work of making disciples, and He was pleased to present them to the Father. But this was not the completion of His prayer. Thirdly, Jesus prayed for their protection and the fruit of their efforts to make disciples. We see this emphasis in the final words that Jesus had given to the disciples in Galilee:

> All authority in heaven and on earth has been given to me. Go therefore and make disciples of all nations, baptizing them in the name of the Father, Son and the Holy Spirit, teaching them to observe all that I have commanded you. And behold, I am with you always, to the end of the age (Matt. 28:16–20).

The same thing that He promised His disciples (*authority and presence*), He now prayed for them in His prayer to the Father. However, this time, He prayed not only for His disciples but for those who will believe in Christ through their obedience to the Great Commission.

> I do not ask for these only, but also for those who
> will believe in me through their word. (John 17:20)

It appears that Jesus was confident that His disciples would carry out the Great Commission as they were motivated by the great commandment to *love God and love people* (Matt. 22:34–37). This commitment, which was seen in the early church (Acts 2:2–47), is a commitment that should be seen in the church of today. But is it?

I have many wonderful memories of being part of the church over the years, and yet few of them are about the priority of making disciples. I can remember many invitations to a meeting, an announcement encouraging us to please come to this week's revival services, or to not forget to bring extra food for the potluck dinner, *but virtually nothing about what the church is doing to promote the priority of making disciples.*

That which Jesus accomplished through the original disciples, and was intended to continue, even to today, obviously got derailed along the way. Many churches are more focused on their property, programs, or personal priorities than obeying the mandate of making disciples given by Christ. Unfortunately, the more this happens, the further the church moves away from God's design for the church, and the harder it is to get realigned to His purpose for all of us.

PICK THE RIGHT SOLUTION

The answer to our situation as churches is to pick the right solution to our problem. It is not to run more programs, bring more exciting groups into our church, or even find another pastor. No, the solution is to get back to the basics of making disciples who make disciples. Unless this becomes the priority of the church in both belief and practice, there is little hope for the church. The question for the church is, *How do we do it?* There is no better example of how we are to make disciples than *observing* and *obeying* the model given to us by Jesus.

OBSERVING THE PATTERN OF JESUS

Jesus's journey with his disciples began when He called them to be "with" Him (Mark 3:14). I am quite certain that none of the disciples had a clue as to what lay ahead as they entered into a relationship with their *rabbi*, but Jesus knew exactly what He was doing. There was nothing accidental about Jesus's invitation. He knew exactly what He wanted to accomplish and when it would be completed (John 17:4). One can see both the simplicity and the power of Jesus's call to be with Him in His original invitation: "Follow Me and I will make you fishers of men" (Matt. 4:19).

While the New Testament is filled with the content of their recorded adventures, one can only imagine all of the conversations and discussions that took place every day as they moved from place to place. Jesus had a clear and uncomplicated way in which He was going to disciple these men. Yes, He gathered a crowd and preached inspiring messages, but He went much further and on a deeper level with these men along the way.

It is quite interesting to note that Jesus's method of making disciples demonstrated *intentionality*. There was nothing haphazard about how Jesus went about the work of making disciples. He focused on the Twelve, and even one of them didn't make it. Beyond intentionality, the most significant aspect of his disciple-making methodology was the *relational* nature of His plan. In this way, each member of the original twelve was invested in personally. Peter, James, and John were obviously the most engaged in what Jesus was doing on a daily basis; and it appears that John was one that Jesus especially loved (John 13:23; 19:26; 20:2; 21:7, 20). Thomas doubted, and Judas betrayed Him; yet they were all considered (and called) disciples.

Jesus modeled what He *taught*, and the disciples *caught* more than they heard. His plan was simple as Jim Putman states,

> Jesus was going to teach and empower them to be like himself. Jesus was going to address their beliefs (head), their attitudes (heart and character), and actions (hands) as he shaped them into

messengers who would deliver the good news to the world.[51]

OBEYING THE COMMAND OF JESUS

Not only did the early disciples of Christ *observe* what He did, they *obeyed* what He told them to do. The apostle Paul, who was not one of the original twelve disciples, captured the heart of Jesus's process of making disciples. Almost thirty years after the resurrection of Jesus from the dead and the beginning of the early church, Paul continued the method of making disciples by instructing Timothy with these words:

> You then, my child, be strengthened by the grace that is in Christ Jesus, and what you have heard from me in the presence of many witnesses entrust to faithful men who will be able to reach others also (2 Tim. 2:1–2).

This approach to making disciples is amazingly similar to the discovery that Dann Spader made after years of studying the life of Jesus as it is revealed in the New Testament. At the heart of his discovery was the belief that Jesus not only had a *message*; He also had a *method*. Spader wrote: "But I would argue that if you completely understand the message of Christ but fail to understand His methods, you won't truly know the Jesus of the Scriptures. Jesus was much more than just His words and message." [52]

Few people realize that long before Jesus invited the disciples to follow Him so He could turn them into "fishers of men,"[53] Jesus had known them relationally for at least a year and a half. According to

[51.] Jim Putman, *Real-Life Discipleship* (NavPress, PO Box 35001, Colorado Springs, CO 80935), pg. 29–30.
[52.] Dann Spader, *4 Chair Discipling: Growing a Movement of Disciple-Makers* (Moody Publishers, 820 N. LaSalle Boulevard, Chicago, IL 60610), pg. 14.
[53.] Mark 1:17.

the Scriptures (Luke 6:12–16), when Jesus chose the twelve disciples to be with Him, He had known them for two and a half years. Your reaction to this may be the same as that of others who agree that this may be true but balk at the idea that they can do what Jesus did simply because He is God, and we are not. When it comes to understanding the methodology of Jesus in making disciples, the fact that Jesus was fully human is the most important thing of all. We are not asked to do something that only God can do. It makes no sense to think that Jesus would tell His disciples to do something that they could never do. The beauty of Jesus's relationship with His disciples was the fact that He showed them how to be a disciple through His life as a fully human being.

THE IMPACT OF JESUS'S HUMANITY

Have you ever noticed that the things that Jesus talked about in terms of making disciples continue to show up in the words of Paul, Peter, and John, as well as others? Their lives and their writings demonstrate the impact of Jesus's message and methods on them. Over forty times, we are able to see the same thoughts and practices being emphasized. It's not very hard to accept the idea that after spending time with Jesus for over three years; your life would be changed.

Like Jesus (and many more in the early church) were changed by the way that Jesus lived His life. He was faithfully committed to the practice of prayer. Over forty times, Jesus withdrew to a quiet place for the sole purpose of prayer—a time when He could connect with His Father. Over ninety times, Jesus quoted from the Old Testament Scriptures, always connecting the dots between what was written and how it was to be understood and applied to the present. And most importantly, He was led by the Holy Spirit in everything that He did. Read the New Testament again, and make note of all these things. It is no wonder that the disciples of Jesus never forgot them.

ALL YOU NEED IS LOVE

The Apostle John was led to write five books in the New Testament. Each book is filled with statements about the importance of love. In the gospel, he makes it clear that "God so loved the world, that he gave his only Son, that whoever believes in him should not perish but have eternal life" (John 3:16). In his Epistles (1 and 2 John), we see him commending the church for their expressions of love:

> Beloved, it is a faithful thing you do in all your efforts, strangers as they are, who testified to your love before the church. (3 John 5)

> Now I ask you, dear lady-not as though I were writing you a new commandment, but that we love one another. And this is love that we walk according to his commandments, just as you have heard from the beginning, so that you should walk in it. (2 John 5–6)

In John's first Epistle, more than anywhere else, we see how the love of Jesus impacted his life and the practice of his faith. John writes:

> Beloved, let us love one another, for love is from God and whoever loves has been born of God and knows God. Anyone who does not love does not know God, because God is love. In this the love of God was made manifest among us, that God sent his only Son into the world, so that we might live through him. In this is love, not that we have loved God but that he loved us and sent his Son to be the propitiation for our sins. Beloved, if God so loved us, we ought to love one another. No one has ever seen God; if we

love one another, God abides in us and his love is
perfected in us. (1 John 4:7–12)

One would have to be blind not to notice the emphasis that is
made by John on the importance of love. Later in this same passage,
he summarized the impact of God's love on his life with this statement: "We love because he first loved us" (1 John 4:19). John had felt
the love of Jesus and even spoke of it in his own gospel material (John
13:23). It is worth noting that in addition to the truth proclaimed
and heard by John coming from Jesus, it was the sense that he was
loved that made a life-changing impact.

THE NITTY-GRITTY OF A DISCIPLED PERSON

During the years of 1951 to 1959, NBC produced a TV show
called *Dragnet*. The show took its name from the police term *dragnet*, a system of coordinated measures for apprehending criminals or
suspects. The show was shot in Los Angeles, where Joe Friday and his
partners methodically investigated crimes.

Anyone who watched the show became familiar with a common phrase used to sharpen the focus of their investigation. Friday
was often heard saying, "Just the facts, ma'am, just the facts." I can't
help but think that when Paul advised young Timothy in his second
letter to entrust what he had seen and heard through the life of Paul
to reliable men so that they could teach others, he was giving him *just
the facts* (2 Tim. 2:1–2).

A CONTEMPORARY APPROACH

A pastor will not be hard-pressed to find many ideas about making disciples in the twenty-first century. However, the actual condition of most churches today suggests that they do not have a plan.
The reality is this: *if they do not have a plan, they have a plan, and it is
a plan to fail.* With this fact in mind, I want to share an approach to
disciple-making that is both biblical and practical.

First, the plan to make disciples must be *relational*. That is, the disciple-maker must prioritize spending time with those he or she seeks to disciple. I am not talking about casual connections but rather, *intentional* effort to spend time with your disciple. The miscellaneous activities of leading the church must take a back seat to building relationships with people who are going to carry on the work of making disciples who make disciples.

Secondly, *the plan must engage the Scriptures, and guide the disciples as to how they are to live their lives in obedience to the commands of the Lord*. This plan must not only be biblical, it must be practical and with evidence of how one is to do it. They must not only understand it and be able to teach others what the Scriptures say, they must learn how to model it in all that they do.

Thirdly, *the plan must be something that everyone can relate to as they continue on their journey toward becoming a disciple-maker*. We all know that some people learn better by seeing an example, while others can get a mental picture through reading. We are all different, but as seen in the life of the Apostle John, not everyone is impacted with the truth in the same way. For this reason, I want to share a model of learning that a disciple-maker can use to engage a person as they grow in their understanding of what it means to be a disciple. Years back, when I first began to work on this model, the term **Description of a Discipled Person (DDP)** was used. I see no reason to abandon or change it today.

DESCRIPTION OF A DISCIPLED PERSON[54]

I have found that by building a picture of a fully devoted follower of Christ, the use of an acronym[55] is helpful. It only seemed right to use the word *DISCIPLE* as my choice. By using this model,

---

[54.] This entire DDP (Description of a Discipled Person) was developed by Dr. Sam Warren while serving as pastor of the West Jacksonville Advent Christian Church from 1989–2006.

[55.] An abbreviation formed from the initial letters of other words and pronounced as a word (disciple).

a person can be exposed to the godly characteristics seen in a variety of biblical characters and be given the opportunity to measure those qualities in their lives. Through the leading of the Holy Spirit, persistent prayer, and adherence to these examples of what it means to be a disciple, a person can grow in their own spiritual maturity to the point where they can join the process of passing it on to someone else.

As you begin your journey, ask God to open your eyes and heart to how He wants to shape or reshape your thoughts and actions as a follower of Christ. I am confident of this one thing, as Paul was with the Philippians, "that he who began a good work in you will bring it to completion at the day of Jesus Christ" (Phil. 1:6).

Daily Devoted to God in Christ
Instructed by the Word of God
Spirit-Filled and-Led
Conforming to the Image of Christ
Impacting Others for Christ
Participating in the Body through Giftedness
Loving Others
Evangelistic in Purpose

Daily Devoted to God in Christ
Key Passages: 1 Corinthians 7:35; 2 Corinthians 11:3; Titus 3:8
Personification: Jesus
Description: A person committed to serving Christ daily in every aspect of life.
Measured by:

1. A deep understanding and thankfulness for Christ's sacrifice on the cross.
2. A commitment to use one's giftedness toward the furthering of God's kingdom.
3. A contagious joy in giving oneself away to others in ministry for Christ.
4. Determined to sacrificially serve God in all areas of one's life.

Instructed by the Word of God
Key Passages: Colossians 3:16; 2 Timothy 2:15, 3:16; James 1:22; Acts 17:11
Personification: The Bereans
Description: A person who grows in biblical knowledge and applies it to their daily living.
Measured by:

1. A dynamic understanding of the inspiration, inerrancy, and authority of the Bible.
2. Able to personally and correctly apply God's Word to everyday life and decision-making.
3. Personally committed and devoted to an ongoing study of the Bible.
4. Committed to studying the Word of God with others.

Spirit-Filled and Spirit-Led
Key Passages: Galatians 5:16–18; Ephesians 5:18–19
Personification: Paul
Description: A person who seeks the guidance of the Holy Spirit and tries to apply the truth to their lives daily.
Measured by:

1. Understanding the purpose and work of the Holy Spirit in a disciple's life.
2. Possessing the ability to discern between the power of the flesh and the power of the spirit
3. Demonstrating the joy of the spirit through the fruit of the spirit.
4. Regularly seeking the leading of the Holy Spirit in the development of new relationships with those who do not know Christ personally.

Conforming to the Image of Christ
Key Passages: Romans 8:29, Romans 12:1–2
Personification: Timothy

Description: A person who is experiencing the transforming power of God's presence in their life on a daily basis.

Measured by:

1. Understanding that our ultimate goal is to become more like Christ each and every day.
2. Using the disciplines that God provides for us to become more like Him.
3. An attitude of expectancy over what God is going to do in and through my life.
4. Modeling the changes God is making in my life to those He puts me in contact with on a daily basis.

Impacting Others for Christ

Key Passages: 1 John 3:16–18; 1 Timothy 4:15–16; 1 John 4:20–21

Personification: Daniel

Description: A person who shares their time, talent, and finances for God's work and purposes.

Measured by:

1. A keen sense that one has been blessed to be a blessing.
2. Effectively budgets their finances, time, and talents for the blessings of others and the glory of God.
3. Possesses a cheerful and generous heart.
4. Makes quiet yet generous contributions that help the poor and further the work of the local church.

Participating in the Body through Giftedness

Key Passages: 1 Corinthians 12:4–11; Ephesians 4:12–13

Personification: Barnabas

Description: A person who uses their spiritual gift for the building up of the body and encourages others to do the same.

Measured by:

1. A belief that God has given each believer at least one spiritual gift to be used in and through the body.
2. An ability to encourage the body through word and deed.
3. A genuine desire to see others use their gifts for the glory of God.
4. Regularly seeks opportunities to help others in need through the use of their gift.

Loving Others
Key Passages: Matthew 19:19; John 13:34
Personification: John
Description: A person who unconditionally and proactively loves people with the love of Christ.
Measured by:

1. A deep understanding and gratitude for the love of God demonstrated in the life and death of Christ.
2. A creative approach to showing the love of Christ to others in word and in deed.
3. Unreservedly giving oneself to the needs of others.
4. A strategic effort to unselfishly communicate the love of Christ to people in your life.

Evangelistic in Purpose
Key Passages: Matthew 28:16–20
Personification: Andrew
Description: A person who implements a strategic plan and passion for reaching his friends, peers, and family for Christ.
Measured by:

1. Managing time in a way that prioritizes solid relationships with lost people.
2. Explaining the gospel simply and lovingly.

3. Demonstrates a sincere compassion for lost people.
4. Is known as a friend of spiritually lost people.

As the journey continues, now more than ever, we find that the relationships that we build with people become our most important effort. This will now be the focus of our discussion.

CHAPTER 7

A BIG DO-OVER

A disciple is a person who has decided that
the most important thing in their life is to learn
how to do what Jesus said to do.

—Dallas Willard

The first ministers were the twelve disciples.
There is no evidence that Jesus chose them because they
were brighter or nicer than other people. Their sole
qualification seems to have been their initial willingness
to rise to their feet when Jesus said, "Follow Me."

—Frederick Buechner

My grandson recently turned three years old, and of course, I love him even more than I thought I would. Friends always told me that it was great fun to watch them grow up, spoil them as much I could, and then give them back to their parents. I must say that they were right.

What I didn't count on was having to deal with his independent spirit and typical response of "it's mine" to almost everything. I must admit that many of his mannerisms are very cute and give us a reason to laugh. However, he's a three-year-old. What's funny now will cease to be humorous in a few years as he matures.

Trying to change his behavior can sometimes be very challenging when little has been attempted to teach him the right way. This is even difficult for an adult. Recently, I read an article that suggested that it takes a lot more than the mythical 21 or 28 days to establish a new habit. According to the *European Journal of Psychology* and the work of psychologist Phillippa Lally, it takes at least 66 days to establish a new habit.[56] Some participants in her study took up to 245 days to establish a new habit. This leaves little doubt as to why people rarely change their behavior even when it's detrimental to themselves or to others. Without the persistent practice of a new habit, little can be expected to change.

Imagine adults who have lived their entire lives a certain way but now are hearing that it is possible to live differently. Unfortunately, according to the report of Stephanas, Fortunatus, and Achaicus (1 Cor. 15:1–18), things weren't going so well. Much of their behavior in Paul's absence was demonstrating their lack of spiritual maturity (1 Cor. 3:1) even though they were Christians. Upon Paul's return to Corinth, he was surprised to find out how many of the believers were still *spiritual infants* (1 Cor. 3:1).

No surprise that the books of 1 and 2 Corinthians are filled with Paul's teaching on many subjects related to living an authentic and God-filled life. Given the culture of Corinth, anything less would be disastrous for the church and the advancement of the gospel.

When one takes a closer look at the condition of the contemporary church, it becomes quite clear that we, too, should be more mature in our faith than we are. This immaturity shows up in our man-centered worship, lack of biblical teaching, potluck approach to fellowship, and me-centered prayer. Not to mention the fact that the primary mandate of *making disciples*, which was given to the church by Christ, is almost nonexistent.

[56.] Phillippa Lally, *European Journal of Psychology* (John Wiley & Sons, 2009. Edited by Roland Imhoff, Joanne Smith, and Martijn Zomeren).

A BIG DO-OVER

Billy Graham was one of the greatest, if not the greatest, evange-lists the world has ever known. It's quite possible that he preached the gospel to more people in his lifetime than anyone else. Nevertheless, it was during his experience as an evangelist that he learned, perhaps the most important lesson of all.

Nearing the end of his ministry, Billy was asked what lessons he had learned over the years, and if he could do it all over again, what would he do differently? His answer was very surprising. He said, "If I could do it all over again, I would prayerfully select twelve men to be with me. I would spend my time with them and share with them all that God has taught me. Then, I would set them free to do the same with others."[57]

What's truly amazing about Billy's answer to this question is the fact that in my lifetime, there is no one I can think of that made a bigger impact on the spiritual lives of people than Billy Graham. And yet he would do a do-over. Of course, this can't happen, especially since Billy is no longer with us. However, it's not too late for the church. We can start over in our effort to make disciples. A friend once told me, "It's never too late to begin to do things the way Christ wants us to do them."

TOPOGRAPHICALLY DISORIENTED

The next time my wife, Shelly, and I are traveling somewhere and she suggests that we are not going the right way, I might just use this term on her. Why do I say that? Well, let me put it this way: when I need help navigating my way on a journey, I need more input than "this doesn't feel right."

It seems that the local church of today suffers from a big dose of this condition. When someone makes the point that we should

---

[57]. It was during a campus visit from Billy Graham at Gordon-Conwell Theological Seminary (where I went to graduate school) that I heard him asked this question and give this response.

do something differently, many argue that it's not the way that we've always done it; therefore, it just doesn't feel right. If we are going to fulfill the work of making disciples that was given to us by Jesus, it will be necessary for us to begin a new habit of behavior that will lead to our obedience of His command, and I am confident that it will *feel just right.*

STARTING OUT RIGHT

My friend Dr. David Ferguson[58] is the first one to drive home the experience of *aloneness* to me. It was in the garden of Eden that it all began. Everything was good until Adam was created. Even though Adam lived in a perfect world, possessed everything that he could possibly need or want, had an exalted position over the created world, and enjoyed an intimate relationship with God, it wasn't enough. Ferguson argues that Adam was created perfectly; yet he was still needy. His comments are based on Genesis 2:18, which states, "It is not good for the man to be alone."

While Adam's needs, physical and spiritual, were met through his relationship with God, his need for human relationship was not.[59] As we know, this need was met through the creation of Eve (Gen. 2:18–25), and it continues to be a need throughout life and ministry for each of us.

Man was never created to be alone. His need for relationships can only be met through God and another human being.

A RELATIONAL THREAD

One can hardly miss the presence of a need for relationships woven throughout the entire Bible. We see it in terms of leadership. God often called another person to come alongside a leader to help them carry out his work (Aaron, Joshua, Jonathan, the disciples,

---

58. Founder of the Great Commandment Network located in Cedar Park, Texas.
59. David Ferguson, *The Never Alone Church* (Tyndale House Publishers, Wheaton, IL, 1998), pg. 25–26.

Timothy, Titus, etc.). Paul established a plurality of elders in the early church (1 Tim. 5:17) and ministry leaders for the equipping of the saints to do the work of the church (Eph. 4:11–14). In order to carry out the Great Commission, Timothy was instructed to *entrust* the things that he had heard Paul say to men who would be able to teach others (1 Tim. 2:1–2). To neglect the importance of working through relationships in an effort to accomplish the work of the church is to forsake the Lord's plan to make disciples.

I wonder if Timothy knew how to do this. Did he know the criteria for being a faithful man? In what way would he pass these truths on to these men, already knowing that there were some who looked down on him because of his youth (1 Tim. 4:11)? We know this much: his approach was to be the key to the health and success of his ministry in Ephesus.

GETTING STARTED

Have you ever thought about how Timothy started the process of passing on the things that he had learned from Paul to reliable men? Would a group of older men be receptive to a young man telling them how ministry was to be done? Or is it more likely that Timothy would begin by initiating relationships with individual men in the hope that one day they would turn into a group of faithful men who would be ready to lead the ministry, guided by sound doctrine and the experience of the Apostle Paul to guide them?

Keith Phillips reminds us in his book *The Making of a Disciple*. Keith Phillips reminds us that true disciple-making is a *life on life encounter.*[60]

The end goal is to produce another disciple. Phillips writes: "No person is an end in himself. Every disciple is part of a process, part of God's chosen method for expanding His kingdom through reproduction."[61] The opportunity to begin a relationship with a potential

---

[60.] Keith Phillips, *The Making of a Disciple* (Fleming H. Revell Company, Old Tappan, New Jersey, 1981), pg. 101.

[61.] Ibid., pg. 21.

disciple may take time, so until then, Timothy was charged to carry out his ministry in this way:

> Command and teach these things. Let no one despise you for your youth, but set the believers an example in speech, in conduct, in love, in faith, in purity. Until I come, devote yourself to the public reading of the Scripture, to exhortation, to teaching. Do not neglect the gift you have, which was given you by prophecy when the council of elders laid their hands oh you. Practice these things, immerse yourself in them, so that all my see your progress. Keep a close look on yourself and on the teaching. Persist I this, for by so doing you will save both yourself and your hearts (1 Tim. 3:11–16).

Again, Phillips writes:

> A disciple employs a gift or talent that builds the kingdom or edifies the body. He confidently refrains from exercising abilities that might destructively foster his pride or hinder his Christian maturity. A dead man's focus is on God. He seeks to be like Christ.
>
> If any man had a reason to find security in his reputation, abilities or credentials it was the apostle Paul. Yet he realized that these were rubbish compared to becoming like Christ (Phil. 3:8). **A person's skill is worthless without a godly character.**[62]

Little would be accomplished if Timothy's lack of character prevented others from listening to the truths that he wanted to share

---

[62] Phillips, ibid., pg. 36.

with them. It is clear from the context of this imperative ("entrust") that was given to Timothy that this had to be his number one focus during his ministry in Ephesus. Like a soldier who can't get entangled in civilian affairs (1 Tim. 2:2b), an athlete who must compete according to the rules (2 Tim. 2:5), or the hardworking farmer who works for a fruitful harvest from the field (2 Tim. 2:6), Timothy was to be singularly focused on the work of making disciples. He must make the imperative of *entrusting* the things that Paul had taught him to reliable men his number one priority.

WHAT COULD HAPPEN?

This was not the first time that Timothy was told to *entrust* or "put before"[63] the brothers the words of the faith and the doctrine that he had followed much of his life (1 Tim. 4:6, 2 Tim. 3:15). But it was the first time that he was told to implement a disciple-making process that would continue Paul's work (and more specifically, the church's work) of making disciples who would make disciples.

As the journey toward becoming a disciple begins, Timothy must find people who are willing to count the cost. Jesus put it this way:

> If anyone comes to me and does not hate his own father and mother and wife and children and brothers and sisters, yes and even his own life, he cannot be my disciple. Whoever does not bear his own cross and come after me cannot be my disciple. For which of you, desiring to build a tower, does not first sit down and count the cost, whether he has enough to complete it? Otherwise, when he has laid a foundation and is not able to finish, all who see it begin to mock him, saying, "This man began to build and was not able to finish." Or what king, going out to encounter another

---

63. Entrust or put before (υποτιθεμενοσ).

84

king in war, will not sit down first and deliberate whether he is able with ten thousand to meet
him who comes against him with twenty thousand? And if not, while the other is yet a great way
off, he sends a delegation and asks for terms of
peace. So therefore, any one of you who does not
renounce all that he has cannot be my disciple.[64]

This passage from the Bible has scared me for years. It seems
kind of drastic. Does Jesus mean that I have to literally hate my parents, friends, and even myself if I am going to become a disciple?
Not really! However, it is clear that Jesus is looking for depth in our
commitment to Him. When things get tough (and life can be that
way), He demands that we keep our hand to the plow (Luke 9:62).

Nowadays, pastors have great difficulty approaching the disciple-making process in this way. We don't want to be pushy as we get to
know people. Our questions, while seemingly harmless, perpetuate a
shallow connection with people that we are called to disciple. Clearly
Jesus understood this as He could have invited the disciples to join
Him on a tour of Israel. They were natives of the land, so they could
have shown Him things that He had never seen before. Instead, after
being exposed to them for two and a half years, He challenged them
to join Him so He could make them "fishers of men" (Luke 5:10b).

I am not totally convinced that they knew what He was talking
about. They were fishermen, so I'm sure that they connected on some
level. Nevertheless, having heard Jesus on occasion (and no doubt
were interested in his message), they responded immediately when
He called to them. Interestingly, the Bible says "they left everything
and followed Him" (Luke 5:11).

Part of the challenge for every pastor and leader is the temptation to dumb down[65] the invitation to enter a relationship for the
purpose of becoming a disciple.

[64.] Luke 14:26–33.

[65.] To lower the level of difficulty and the intellectual content of something, like
what it will take to become a disciple.

THE SHACKLETON SAGA

On August 3, 1913, a Canadian expedition led by Vilhjalmur Stefansson set out to explore the frozen Arctic, between the northernmost shores of Canada and the North Pole. On December 5, 1914, the British Imperial Trans-Antarctic Expedition, led by Sir Ernest Shackleton, sailed from the island of South Georgia in the Southern Ocean. Its goal was the first overland crossing of Antarctica.

Both ships, (the *Karluk* in the north and the *Endurance* in the south) soon found themselves beset in the solid ice. Trapped by the ice, each crew was soon engaged in a fight for survival. But the outcomes of these two adventures—and the ways in which the two leaders dealt with the obstacles they faced were as far apart as the poles each leader set out to explore.[66]

For the *Karluk,* a lack of leadership and teamwork led to tragic consequences for 11 members of its crew; but the 27-member crew of the *Endurance* survived the 684-day trip, which ended on August 30, 1916. If the truth be told, the success of this adventure began with the invitation to get on board. It all began with an advertisement that appeared in the London papers:

> Men wanted for Hazardous Journey. Small wages, bitter cold long months of complete darkness, constant danger, safe return doubtful. Honour and recognition in case of success.[67]

[66.] Dennis N. T. Perkins, *Leading at the Edge* (American Management Association, New York, NY, 2000) pg. 13.

[67.] *Leading at the Edge*, pg. 2.

The ability of individuals to work with others was clearly on his mind from the beginning. For example, when interviewing Reginald James, who later became the expedition's physicist, he asked whether the prospective scientist could sing. He was not, however, probing for vocal ability. In asking whether James could "shout a bit with the boys," Shackleton was undoubtedly looking to see if James could live and work with others in close quarters under difficult conditions.

With some notable exceptions, Shackleton seemed to have largely succeeded in selecting a group of people who had the capacity to work together. But he clearly did not select a homogeneous group that could be expected to gel of its own accord. There was a diverse mix of temperaments: some cheerful and gregarious, others introverted and reserved. There were physicians, scientists, seamen, and artists. Shackleton did not simply assume that teamwork would happen.[68]

Shackleton's group sounds incredibly just like the original twelve disciples chosen by Jesus. It was quite a diverse gathering of men as well. There were fishermen, a tax collector, a zealot, and a traitor, Judas Iscariot, who betrayed Him. They couldn't have been more different; yet these are the men that Jesus chose to carry out His mission.

Just as Jesus, Shackleton and Timothy each had to set the stage for what He wanted to do with these men. We, as pastors, must select and prepare our potential disciples for the exciting but challenging work to be done.

I don't know much about the type of people that made up the church in Ephesus, but Timothy's work had begun. Perhaps he spent

---

[68.] *Leading at the Edge*, pg. 71.

the night in prayer, like Jesus did before He confronted the men of choice. Now that he had some men to entrust with the teachings of Paul, one must wonder exactly what they were.

What could young Timothy hope to teach these men that would be worth passing on to others (2 Tim. 2:1–2) and how would he teach them? A careful reading of Paul's letters will reveal some surprising answers.

RELATIONAL NUTRIENTS

I certainly do not have a green thumb, but I understand this agricultural principle: good fruit comes from trees planted in good soil (Matt. 13:23). Jesus used this image in John 15, verse 5 when he said,

> I am the vine; you are the branches. Whoever abides in e and I in him, he it is that bears much fruit, for apart from me you can do nothing

Timothy was to "put before" faithful men the things that Paul had taught him. This means he was to put these things in the care and protection of these men so they could pass them on to others,[69] which means that he was charged to lay before these men the truths of God's Word that he had heard from Paul. The selection of faithful men implies that these men were human examples of "good soil" that would produce much fruit in others.

Respected Christian psychologist John Townsend points out in his new book, *People Fuel,* that there are three fruit categories by which all of us measure our lives, happiness, and success which he calls the three Ps (Personal, People, and Performance). The third P is a life or ministry of good performance fruit. For the pastor or leader in the church, this would be making disciples.[70] He goes on to say

---

[69.] Παραθου, which literally means "to put in care of or protection of someone."
[70.] John Townsend, *People Fuel* (Zondervan, 3900 Sparks Dr. SE, Grand Rapids, MI 49546), pg. 44–49.

that when we don't see the healthy fruit being produced, we don't "yell at the fruit."[71] Townsend states, "A great majority of the time, we can't blame the fruit. It's only as good as the soil ingredients."[72]

Townsend's extensive study of relationships shows that there are *relational nutrients* that are necessary for the health of the soil, whether it's soil in the ground or in the heart of a man. Interestingly, these nutrients fall into what Townsend calls 4 Quadrants: *Be Present, Convey the Good, Provide Reality,* and *Call to Action.*[73] Like the physical soil in which we plant seeds to grow, the discipler must prepare the soil of a disciple in a certain way so that he can grow and mature resulting in more disciples.

DISCIPLING NUTRIENTS

Just as the soil and people in general need nutrients to grow, disciples must have certain biblical nutrients to turn their hearts and minds into good soil. To the Christians in Rome, Paul put it this way:

> I appeal to you therefore, brothers, by the mercies of God, to present your bodies as a living sacrifice holy and acceptable to God which is your spiritual worship. Do not be conformed to this world but **be transformed by the renewing of your mind** that by testing you may discern what is the will of God, what is good and acceptable and perfect. (Rom. 12:1–2)

First and foremost, these men must be believers who have confessed their sin of falling short of God's glory (Rom. 3:23) and are justified (made right with God [Rom. 3:24]) by His grace. Paul was concerned about men who aspire to serve in leadership roles without

---

71. Ibid., pg. 48.
72. Ibid., pg. 49.
73. Ibid., pg. 81.

having proven the presence of God in their lives by the way they live (1 Tim. 3:1–13).

Rather than be shaped by influences on the outside, which is *conformation,* believers are to be *transformed from the inside out* (in essence), and simply put, biblical conformation is inner transformation. What then are the inner nutrients needed by Timothy to pass on to faithful men so that they can do the same? Let's take a look!

SOUND DOCTRINE

Years ago, my dad helped me build and erect a privacy fence around our new home. I was his right-hand man. I mean, I handed him a board or hammered a nail into place. My father, however, did all the hard work. That is, he made sure that the boards were properly aligned vertically and horizontally.

Now, years later, I have discovered that there are fancy tools like lasers available to do the same thing. My father used something his father had taught him to use. It wasn't fancy, but it was amazingly effective. What was it, you ask? It was a string with an arrowhead tied to the bottom of the string. He would hang it in the appropriate place each time he needed to make certain of the alignment. The end result was a beautiful fence perfectly erected with a simple tool and a lot of hard work.

It might be helpful to remember at this time that much of what Timothy knew about what it means to serve God was passed on by Paul and the apostles. Of course, there was a need to recall and understand much of the Old Testament, but this didn't mean that they didn't sat down and read a Bible. No, their discussion was face-to-face, making sure that what they were in agreement with was what they heard.

That's what's missing today: a type of biblical Socratic discussion that can help each of us understand the truth of God's Word and be able to pass it on to others without blatant misinterpretation and application. For this reason, Timothy was to do his very best (spoudason); that is, to be diligent at rightly handling the word of truth (2 Tim. 2:15) in order to help his disciples do the same.

Abraham Lincoln once said, "You have to know where you are going. To be able to state it clearly and concisely. And you have to care about it passionately. That all adds up to vision." An effective vision empowers people and prepares for the future while also having roots in the past. Everywhere Lincoln went, at every conceivable opportunity, he reaffirmed, reasserted, and reminded everyone of the basic principles on which the nation was founded. His vision was simple, and he repeated it often.[74]

This was exactly what Timothy had to do with his *faithful men.* He was to remind them of the story of God's faithfulness in the past, as well as in the present. He was to teach them of the consistency and soundness of God's Word and how they were to depend on the Holy Spirit to guide them in the use of it (Eph. 6:17). He could not force it on them, for an effective vision and mission can't be forced upon anyone; it must be set in motion by means of *persuasion.*[75]

Armed with the truthfulness of God's Word, Timothy's men could now focus on the condition of their lives, knowing that even if they knew the truth, people would not accept them or their message if the way they lived contradicted it.

UNHYPOCRITICAL LIVING

Billy Graham once stated that he suspected that at least 50 percent of all people sitting in church on a Sunday morning were lost spiritually. One might wonder why he would make such a drastic statement. Could it be due to the fact that many lost people are not interested in God simply due to what they see in the lives of those who say that they are Christians?

In 2007, David Kinnaman and Gabe Lyons wrote a book called *unChristian: What a New Generation Thinks about Christianity* based on the findings of a Barna Group survey. The results were perhaps startling at that time, but in today's world, one might not be sur-

[74.] Donald T. Phillips, *Lincoln on Leadership* (Warner Books, 1271 Avenue of the Americas, New York, NY 10020, 1992), pg. 162–63.
[75.] Donald T. Phillips, *Lincoln on Leadership*, pg. 164.

prised to read about the thoughts of nonbelievers when it comes to Christians.

Discovering that spiritually lost people think that Christians are *hypocritical, judgmental, and more* could go a long way in understanding how difficult it is to reach people with the claims of Christ. If this is true, it is even more disturbing to realize that the making of disciples who make disciples is knocked off track due to the fact that the people doing the making are not genuine.

Interestingly, this is the very point at which we find Timothy to be a great example of how a disciple-maker must live. No wonder Paul was willing to leave him in Ephesus, where he would be given the task of dealing with false teachers (Eph. 1:3ff). It was his *unhypocritical* faith that made all the difference (1 Tim. 1:5 and 2 Tim. 1:5).

Paul's description of Timothy as being unhypocritical is very insightful in terms of becoming an effective disciple-maker. Borrowing from a term used in the theater, Timothy is like an actor that has taken off the mask that allows him to portray a character in a play. With the mask, he sends the message that he is something other than who he really is. With the mask off, he is genuine and represents the *real* Timothy. What he says can be trusted. What he does is not second-guessed. He is genuine and sincere.

A CLOSER LOOK

What would this look like today? According to Kinnaman and Lyons, people who don't really know Christians personally can only draw their conclusions from what they see and hear. When a preacher says that a believer must be faithfully committed to praying but prays little himself, does he wear a mask? If a teacher states that a believer must study their Bible diligently but rushes each week to teach a lesson, one for which he has spent little time studying himself, could it be that he is wearing a mask? When a group of Christians tout the idea of loving people unconditionally but demonstrate their prejudices through the way they treat certain people, is it possible they are wearing masks?

For Timothy to pass on his faith to a group of reliable and faithful men, he must give them no reason to doubt his message. We must take off the mask of trying to impress people with what we know and become passionate about revealing who we are and how we, too, need the transforming power of God in our life. Armed with the soundness of God's Word and the unhypocritical vessel of our life, the true disciple-maker helps his disciple pursue the *righteousness of God*.

THE *RIGHT* APPROACH TO LIVING

Have you ever played the game called *Word Trip* on your phone? It is very addictive. The rules are simple. A few letters are provided from which you are to create words that will fill in the boxes that have been provided. When you get them all, the game is complete. The strategy of the game is to keep going until you fill in all of the boxes. To aid the player, the letters can be arranged differently in the hope that you will see the possibility of a new word which might fill in the blanks.

I must admit that I don't give up that easily. I can stare at those letters for a long time, hoping that I will soon see my missing word. I have even saved the game and come back to it on another day. Perhaps a rested body and mind will open me up to seeing something I couldn't see before. Many times, this works.

In one sense, I think that this is what Paul wanted Timothy to do when he told him to "pursue righteousness, godliness, faith, love, steadfastness, gentleness" (1 Tim. 6:11). You may not find it immediately, since knowing how to think about something or understanding what you should do isn't always clear; keep pursuing it until it is revealed to you. As Paul would advise Timothy in his second letter, "Think over what I say, for the Lord will give you understanding in everything" (Tim. 2:7).

What Paul instructed Timothy to do is not easy. He would face many situations in his ministry that would test his resolve to keep up the pursuit of these characteristics. If Timothy was going to be effective, each of these qualities would have to be present and active not only when he is alone, but more importantly, when he was with his faithful men.

As a believer in Christ, Timothy was commanded to pursue *righteousness* (which according to the Apostle Paul, would lead to *sanctification* [Rom.6:19]). His commitment to the pursuit of these qualities in the presence of faithful men would not only empower Timothy to carry out the imperative of Paul, it would be a key factor in the equipping of the faithful men to do the same (2 Tim. 2:1–2).

STAYING OR LEAVING?

A few weeks ago, prior to the writing of this chapter, I had an experience that continues to drive home the challenge we all have in the pursuit of righteousness, both in and out of the church. It all happened while I was on a trip for my consulting business called Far More Consulting, Inc.

After a long day of working with a church, I rested a bit before getting something for dinner. Having eaten a late lunch, I decided to go eat around eight o'clock. I eventually landed on the idea of eating some wings at a local restaurant. I figured it must be a good place since I could barely find a parking space.

I entered the restaurant and was immediately greeted by a young lady who led me to a high-top table a few feet from the bar area. It was one of the few seats open. As I settled into my seat and began to look at the menu, it became clear to me that this was a different kind of place than I was used to eating my meals at.

The first clue that I was out of my element was the way most (if not all) of the waitresses were dressed (using the word *dressed* would be a real stretch). They were dressed very provocatively. Very little was left to the imagination; their breasts were almost hanging out, and their shorts were more like bikini bathing suits than anything else. You might imagine what I was thinking, or not.

I sat there for a few minutes and wondered if I should leave. The music was loud, the conversations around me were off-color, and most of the time, I didn't know where to look. As I think back on this experience, I realize that it was part of God's plan for me that night to live my faith through a brief relationship with my waitress. I was blessed, I think, as my particular waitress was *pregnant* and covered much more modestly than the other girls.

As I ate my meal, I pondered what I might do. I sensed the nudge of the Holy Spirit to talk with my waitress and ask her a few questions. I didn't want to get too personal or forward, but I did want to talk with her about what I sensed about the staff (and in particular, her employer). So at the right time, I asked a question.

She seemed nice and a little taken back when I asked if I could ask her a personal question. The look on her face told me that she wasn't quite sure but she agreed. I took a breath and told her that I was concerned about how the staff was dressed. Specifically, I asked, "Are any of the girls who work here bothered with how they are made to dress?"

She said, "A few but not many. In fact," she said, "I used to work at a gentlemen's club."

So this wasn't so bad for her.

When she came back to my table with my bill, she picked up right where we left off and asked me, "Why did you ask that question?"

Here was my chance, so I said, "I just have concerns about a boss or establishment that cares more about making money than having respect for the ones who do the work of making money for them."

As we continued to talk, I told her that I was going to pray not only for her baby but for all of the staff that worked in the restaurant.

I didn't know if I had offended her by going too far in the sharing of my thoughts as she stood in front of me for more than a few seconds. I could see her eyes welling up, and her bodily demeanor change. Then she quietly shared these words with me: "Mister, you're one of the few people I know that thinks like you do. Thank you for your willingness to talk with me about this. I won't forget it!

WE ARE NOT JUST PASSING THROUGH

Pursuing righteousness is not a hobby for believers in Christ; it requires a full-time effort on our part. The need to make *righteous* decisions will happen all the time as we make that our focus. I do not know what might come from my conversation with the waitress in my story, but I do know that it was the right thing to do, and that God honored my commitment to Him on that night.

Timothy's faithful men were going to observe his every move, and those who are in relationship with us will do the same. Armed with *sound doctrine, an unhypocritical faith,* and *a commitment to pursue righteousness,* one more thing becomes essential to complete the process for the making of disciples. Timothy must have a *plan of action.* He must *preach the Word.*

WHAT SEASON IS IT?

As Paul completes the writing of what most scholars consider his final letter (2 Tim.), one thing was on his mind. He wanted to make certain that the work of "equipping the saints for the work of the ministry" (Eph. 4:11) would continue through the life of Timothy and those he would equip (2 Tim. 2:1–2).

Each generation of leaders have the responsibility of keeping this work going until Jesus returns (2 Tim. 4:1). Not all will accept what we have to say; therefore, there is a need for you and me to find our faithful men who desire to become disciples and are willing to listen to the Word of God.

These are difficult times for the church, and one of the reasons is the absence of pastors and faithful men who are carrying out the mandate that was given to Timothy by Paul. Something must be done to change the condition of the church toward effective disciple-making. Perhaps a simple biblical and practical plan is what is needed. In the next chapter, we will consider a plan that just might work.

CHAPTER 8

THE MISSING PIECE

You've got to think about big things while
you're doing small things, so that all the small
things go in the right direction.

—Alvin Toffler

Finally, strategy must have continuity. It
can't be constantly reinvented.

—Michael Porter

Imagine for a moment that you live in the first century city of
Ephesus, and you have come into contact with a group of people who
are called Christians. The more you hang around them, the more you
realize that there is something unique or special about them. Their
teachings stir your emotions, mind, and heart.

It all began one day in the marketplace where you meet a young
man named *Timothy*, and you begin a conversation that seemed
different to you. Strangely, you found yourself drawn to him as he
opened up about his life and why he was in Ephesus at that time
(Eph. 6:21). There were things about your conversation that made
you want to know more about this man and the things he said.
Fortunately, he suggested that you meet again to continue your con-

versation, for which you readily agreed. Over the next few weeks, this became a regular habit, which began to impact you in ways you never imagined would happen.

Timothy was becoming a friend. He was kind and gracious as he listened to you ramble on about what was important to you. Yet he was not critical (Eph. 4:29). He said things that made sense and were encouraging. Eventually, as you grew closer, it was hard to resist asking him about his beliefs and why he acted the way he did. However, he was more than willing to take you deeper into what was behind his behavior.

Today was the day. Timothy was taking me to meet some of his friends. He called them *the church*. I didn't really know what that was, but I soon discovered that they were just like him: kind, loving to me, a stranger, and filled with joy. I had to know more, and I was excited to learn the truth.

It was through my relationship with Timothy and the church that I came to know about the one they called Jesus. They told me that before coming to know about Him that they followed the "course of this world" and "the prince of this world" (Eph. 2:1–2), which meant that they lived in pursuit of their fleshly desires (Eph. 2:3). According to a man named Paul, whom I learned about later, we are all "dead in our trespasses and sins" (Eph. 2:10).

I had so much to think about, but something was happening in me after being with the church and hearing them talk about how their lives had changed forever once they came to know Jesus. I had to know more, and once I did, it changed everything for me and my family. Living in Ephesus, I was not unaware of the idea of *gods*. Ephesus itself was the residence of a great temple in honor of *Artemis*,[76] the goddess of the moon, wild animals, and hunting, as

76. Artemis, goddess of the moon, wild animals, and hunting. The cult of Artem is at Ephesus, where she is called Diana by the Romans (Acts 19:23–41) and regarded her especially as a fertility goddess. This was the Greek name of the goddess identified with the Latin Diana of classical mythology. The name Artemis is pre-Greek. She first appears in Greek literature as mistress and pro-tectress of wildlife. (*Cf.* W. K. C. Guthrie, *The Greeks and their Gods*, 1950, pp.

well as the goddess of fertility. An interesting thought since she was considered to be a virgin.

The believers in the church at Ephesus told me how the God of Abraham, Isaac, and Jacob had acted on their behalf by sending His Son, Jesus, to pay the price for our sins, which had caused the separation between God and man. The amazing thing about this message was the fact that God the Father did this even "when we were dead in our trespasses" (Eph. 2:8). The Apostle Paul, who founded the church in Ephesus, put it this way in his letter to the believers:

> By grace you have been saved—and raised us up with him and seated us with him in the heavenly places in Christ Jesus, so that in the coming ages he might show the immeasurable riches of his grace in kindness toward us in Christ Jesus. For by grace you have been saved through faith. And this is not your own doing; it is the gift of God, not a result of works, so that no one may

---

99ff.) In Greece proper, she was worshipped as the daughter of Zeus and Leto, and twin sister of Apollo. Horror at the pains her mother endured at her birth is supposed to have made her averse to marriage. She was goddess of the moon and of hunting and is generally portrayed as a huntress, wild dogs in attendance. Her temple at EPHESUS was one of the Seven Wonders of the World, and here worship of the "virgin goddess" appears to have been fused with some kind of fertility—cult of the mother—goddess of Asia Minor. The temple was supported on one hundred massive columns, some of which were sculptured. Tradition claims that her image fell there from the sky (Acts 19:35) and is thought to refer to a meteorite. Pliny tells of a huge stone above the entrance said to have been placed there by Diana herself. Her worship was conducted by eunuch priests called *megabyzoi* (Strabo, 14. 1. 23), and archaeologists have discovered statues depicting her with many breasts. The silversmiths who made small votary shrines portraying the goddess in a recess with her lions in attendance, or possibly souvenir models of the temple, caused the riot when Paul was ministering there (Acts 19:23–20:1). Their cry of "Great is Artemis of the Ephesians!" (Acts 19:28, 34) is attested by inscriptions from Ephesus which call her "Artemis the Great" (*CIG*, 2963c; *Greek Inscriptions in the British Museum*, iii, 1890, 481. 324).

boast. For we are his workmanship, created in Christ Jesus for good works, which God prepared beforehand that we should walk in them. (Eph. 2:7–10)

As the days and weeks went by, I was able to spend more and more time with the church. This gave me the opportunity to listen to the teaching of Paul and Timothy. It was during this time that I came to faith in Christ. I'm not surprised that this happened, especially after hearing God's message of salvation and how it should impact all of our relationships, including our mates and children.

Like most of my new friends in the church, we are always concerned about the pressure from outside and, in some cases, inside the church to reject the message of Christ in order to pursue some newly formed thought about how you get the most out of life; but for me, it just didn't have a ring of truth. Perhaps it was due to the fact that Paul had written Timothy about the importance of living our lives in accordance to "sound doctrine" (1 Tim. 1:10). I was so excited to find out that God has provided a way to effectively deal with *false teachers* (1 Tim. 11:3–4) and evaluate their myths and genealogies, which promise things it could never provide. Paul's strategy was simple and clear: "Put on the whole armor of God, that you may be able to stand against the schemes of the devil" (Eph. 6:11).

My relationship with Christ and his church has grown to include my wife and children. Every day seems to be a challenge as we are confronted by those who oppose the presence of the church in Ephesus, as well as the message we were trying to share. Thankfully, our task was made clear in Paul's letter to the church:

Therefore, do not become partners with them, for at one time you were darkness, but now you are light in the Lord. Walk as children of light (for the fruit of light is found in all that is good and right and true) and try to discern what is pleasing to the Lord. Take no part in the unfruitful works of darkness, but instead expose them.

> For it is shameful even to speak of the things that
> they do in secret. But when anything is exposed
> by the light, it becomes visible, for anything that
> becomes visible is light. (Eph. 5:7–14a)

And,

> Look carefully then how you walk, not as unwise
> but as wise, making the best use of the time,
> because the days are evil. Therefore, do not be
> foolish, but understand what the will of the Lord
> is. (Eph. 5:15–17)

Somehow, I knew that I was going to need more in my life as I matured in my faith, but how would that happen? You can imagine my surprise when Timothy approached me and told me that due to my faithfulness in Christ, he wanted to spend time with me so he could pass on to me the things that he had learned from Paul and others so that the faith that is found only in Christ might continue to spread to those yet to believe in Christ.

I didn't have any idea what I would learn, but I wanted to know all I could about Christ and what it meant to serve him. Since Timothy asked me to join him in this adventure, I have discovered a few other men who will do the same. I can't wait to get started.

BACK TO THE FUTURE

No matter how much fun it is to imagine life in the first century church, one must always come back to his or her own time and culture. It is clear to me that many things never change. *False teachers* continue to exist and even thrive today. Sadly, the battle against "sound doctrine" finds its way into the church through unbiblical teachings such as a denial of the Triune nature of God or speaking in tongues as a sign of being filled with the Spirit. There will never be an absence of those who claim to know the truth but "have wandered away into vain discussions, desiring to be teachers of the law without understanding either what they are saying or the things about which they make confident assertions" (1 Tim. 1:6–7).

The first time I read Paul's words to Timothy about the "last days" (2 Tim. 3:1) and how sinful people would be, I almost choked. His description could be right out of the twenty-first century.

> But understand this, that in the last days there will come times of difficulty. For people will be lovers of self, lovers of money, proud, arrogant, abusive, disobedient to their parents, ungrateful, unholy, heartless, unappeasable, slanderous, without self-control, brutal, not loving good, treacherous, reckless, swollen with conceit, lovers of pleasure rather than lovers of God, having the appearance of godliness but denying its power. Avoid such people. (2 Tim. 3:1–5)

GOD'S ALTERNATIVE TO A LOST WORLD

Regardless of when or where you live, there will always be those who oppose the church even when they don't know what the church stands for. Many people drive by churches in their community every day and never have a clue what goes on behind the doors. Their upbringing, lifestyles, and interest have never driven them to find out either.

On the other side of the doors sits a people who say that they want to reach the world with the gospel of Jesus but little progress toward that goal ever happens. You may even find a plaque on the wall with Matthew 28:16–20 engraved on it and a mission statement printed in the bulletin, but the gap between the church and the world only widens. Two worlds, side by side, with little interaction and hope of anything changing.

But what might happen if our experience was more like that seen in the imaginary story we began with in this chapter? What would happen if the church was actively engaging the people in their neighborhood, workplace, leisure sites, and anywhere else they go in such a way that would lead them to faith in Christ?

I can't help but think that this was the heartbeat of the early church revealed in the book of Acts 2:42–47. The most amazing thing revealed concerning the early church is the fact that three thousand people could come to faith, and the church knew what to do with them. Insightfully, Peter knew that in order for the young church to survive, they would have to keep themselves *safe* (Greek σωζω) from the "crooked and perverse generation" in which they lived.

Through a commitment to sound doctrine, genuine fellowship, meals centered around the promised return of Christ, worship, and prayer, the early church grew. A sense of awe and unity came over them. They had favor with all the people, but most importantly "the Lord added to their number day by day those who were being saved" (Acts 2:47).

The continued story of the church throughout the Book of Acts reveals the many attacks upon the church from both inside and outside the church. Many of the attacks came from a man named *Saul,* a persecutor of the *Way* (Acts 9:1-19). Following his life-changing encounter on the road to Damascus, Saul would come to faith, be baptized and designated as "God's chosen instrument (of mine) to carry my name before the Gentiles and Kings and the children of God (Acts 9:15). As the journey continued, Saul, *now Paul,* gave a young man named Timothy the opportunity of a lifetime as he would join Paul in the ministry and expansion of the church (Acts 16:1–5).

The fruit of this partnership is seen most clearly in the growth and development of Timothy. Paul's confidence in his young apostolic delegate is best seen in his decision to leave him in Ephesus to lead the church, which was plagued by *false teachers* who had "shipwrecked their faith" (1 Tim. 1:19) and were determined to do the same to others, aptly described as:

> Puffed up with conceit and understands nothing.
> He has an unhealthy craving for controversy and
> for quarrels about words, which produce envy,

dissension, slander, evil suspicions, and constant
friction among people who are depraved in mind
and deprived of the truth, imagining that godliness is a means of gain. (1 Tim. 6:4–6)

The church of the twenty-first century continues to face the
same battles as the church of Ephesus in the first century and the
remedy has never changed. Through the preaching of the Word and
the teaching of sound doctrine to the next generation of believers,
the church will advance to achieve its goal of making disciples and
the passing on of the faith to the next generation until Jesus returns.

THE KEY PIECE THAT IS MISSING

What if the first-century believers came into the twenty-first
century church? Would they be wowed by the size of our facilities,
the music, and perhaps the volume? Would they be taken aback by
the few times we meet for fellowship, study, and worship? How would
they respond to the fact that there are few people who lead and many
who watch and listen? Would they be troubled by seeing the pastor
carrying out the work that others should be doing? How would they
respond to discovering that few people in the church actually know
why the church exists and how they fit into its purpose? I think we
can safely assume that they would be concerned about the condition
of the modern-day church.

On the other hand, if somehow we could travel back in time to
the first century church and experience the life of the early believers,
our hearts would be stirred, and our minds would be enlightened to
see how God intended the church to function. So one might wonder
what went wrong?

THE MISSING PIECE OF THE PUZZLE

Years ago, I worked for days on putting together a one-thou-
sand-piece puzzle, so imagine my reaction to discover that I only
needed one more piece of the puzzle in order to complete it but

couldn't find it. Suddenly, my greatest fear was that I couldn't finish the puzzle because I had lost the last piece. I looked everywhere to find it only to discover a mutilated wet and almost unidentifiable piece in the mouth of my dog. I couldn't believe it. How could I let this happen? How could I not make certain that I had all the pieces to complete the puzzle?

While this memory has stuck in the recesses of my mind, there is definitely a more troubling thing for me to realize as a participant in the church. To be raised in the church and participate in the many activities of the church yet miss the very thing that was intended to make the church healthy and keep it going is the ultimate omission.[77]

As I looked for the puzzle piece many years ago and found that it was right under my feet, it is disappointing to read Paul's final letter to Timothy and discover that the key piece to building an effective and lasting church was there all the time. Nestled in Paul's final communication to Timothy we find these instructions:

> You then, my child be strengthened by the grace that is in Christ Jesus, and what you have heard from me in the presence of many witnesses **entrust** to faithful men who will be able to reach others also. (2 Tim. 2:1–2)

WHAT DID TIMOTHY HEAR?

There's no way to capture in writing all the things that Timothy heard from Paul as he traveled with him on his missionary journeys. And yet one is able to identify a number of things that were priorities for him and anyone given the responsibility of leading the church toward biblical health.

The idea of *entrusting* something to someone means to "put before them" a teaching, a proposed behavior, an insight, and more

---

[77.] To omit the making of disciples as the primary purpose of the church is bad enough. To actually *commit* this omission intentionally is to divert the church away from God's intended purpose.

that will stimulate them to action. Timothy was charged with finding *faithful men* who would be receptive to receiving this kind of instruction. He was to make this his priority and not let anything keep him from making this his practice.

Pastors today are burdened with many expectations as they carry out the work of the pastorate. So much so that the prioritizing of this work is either abandoned or minimized in the midst of all they do. Sadly, this is quite often the missing piece in most churches that prevents them from establishing a solid foundation for future ministry.

Surrounded by a group of men and women who are willing to join Timothy on this journey, it was time to give them the glue that will keep them focused on the right things. It was time to help them understand and accept *sound doctrine* (1 Tim. 1:10). It is no coincidence that much of the turmoil for the church throughout its history has come from those who would seek to lead the church into teachings that are heretical.

Heresy is the choice to abandon the widely accepted teaching on an essential doctrine and embrace one's own view. Those who thought that they could be saved through good works were taught "you are saved through faith, And this is not of your own doing: it is the gift of God, not a result of works, so that no one may boast" (Eph. 2:8–9). Others who preached that it was through the pursuit of riches that they would find contentment were taught that "those who desire to be rich fall into temptation, into a snare, into many senseless and harmful desires that plunge people into ruin and destruction. For the love of money is a root of all kinds of evils. It is through this craving that some have wandered away from the faith and pierced themselves with many pangs" (1 Tim. 6:9–10). The truth of this warning is evidenced by the *prosperity gospel* that is alive and well in the twenty-first century.

Perhaps the foundational truth given by Timothy to his faithful men is the belief in the *inerrancy of the Scriptures.*

> All Scripture is breathed out by God and profitable for teaching, for reproof, for correction, and for training in righteousness, that the man of

God may be complete, equipped for every good work. (2 Tim. 3:16–17)

The rejection of this approach to biblical truth has continued for years. **Rudolf Karl Bultmann** (August 20, 1884–July 30, 1976) was a German theologian of Lutheran background who was, for three decades, a professor of New Testament studies at the University of Marburg. He was one of the founders of form criticism and the primary exponent of *demythologization*, the process of distinguishing the essence of the Christian message from its ancient mythical and miraculous trappings. Only adherence to *sound doctrine* revealed in a careful study of God's written Word could prevent this from happening.

ARMED WITH SOUND DOCTRINE, PURSUING A GENUINE FAITH

As Timothy taught the faithful men the importance of sound doctrine, God was doing a transforming work in their lives. This was true for Timothy as he listened carefully to what Paul had said so many times and in so many places. Timothy's heart and mind were gradually changed into a young man who, like David, was a man after God's own heart (1 Sam. 13:14).

It was easy for Paul to see the change in Timothy's life. He could see the sincere nature of his faith that first lived in his mother and grandmother (2 Tim. 1:4–5). It was an *unhypocritical faith* and one of the primary reasons Paul could leave him in Ephesus to lead the church.

Time spent with faithful men could produce the same fruit. It would not be easy as they confronted the attempts to thwart their faith, but, in the end, they could know that God would do His work in their lives. This is the thought being shared by Paul when he writes:

> If anyone cleanses himself from what is dishonorable, he will be a vessel for honorable use, set apart as holy, useful to the master of the house, ready for every good work. (2 Tim. 2:21)

LEARN, ENCOURAGE, ACHIEVE, DREAM

Thirteen years ago, I began to meet with a group of pastors every three months for an uninterrupted twenty-four-hour period of time. We committed to coming together so we could *pray, study, eat,* and *simply do life together.* We call it the LEAD Team. As a result of our commitment to each other, our lives have been changed. We have become more open and honest with one another, able to share things going on in our lives that are usually tucked away in the protected sections of our minds, more sympathetic and empathetic with each other because we genuinely care. We have prayed about the things that matter to us most rather than the typical prayers uttered even among those who call themselves Christians.

One can only imagine the experience of Timothy and his faithful men as they spent time together over the weeks and months. Like the members of the LEAD Team, not only did they enjoy the relationship forged with each other, they needed it. This is also true for the church of today. The question for the church is an urgent one. Why do we not see this same approach to building the church today?

RELATIONSHIPS THAT REPRODUCE

Why do we keep our distance? Why do we talk about sharing our lives with one another but shy away from getting too close and personal? Could it be because we have not learned to trust each other? One thing is for certain: one will never *entrust* to those he does not *trust.*

We live in a world where it is very difficult to trust each other. We want to know whether we can go deeper in a relationship. Can we be vulnerable? We are looking for those who are *trustworthy,* and this takes time. Jesus knew this from the start. According to Mark, Jesus called the "twelve apostles [together] so that they might be **with him** and he might send them out to preach and have authority to cast out demons (Mark 3:14).

Jesus knew that words would not be enough. He also knew that just being with the Twelve and building a relationship with them would fall short of His goal. The power came from the fact that Jesus not only taught them truth, He lived out the implications of the truth in each relationship. Think about it, Jesus had unique connections to Peter, James, and especially John. He loved Thomas as He challenged him to believe. He loved Judas, who betrayed Him and even washed his feet. I am certain that this was true for the rest of the disciples too.

As Timothy set out to pass on the faith to his faithful men, building relationships that were healthy was his priority. He knew that it might involve reproving, rebuking, or correcting them as this is part of the equipping process. While this was true for Timothy, it is true for each pastor or leader who wants to build a strong and healthy ministry. A personal story from me might drive this thought home for you; it did for me.

After many years of ministry in my last church, I experienced the power of God at work in my relationship with one of the men in the church. It happened as we played in an over forty-year-old basketball league. This night, I received a technical foul in the game, and of course like many players, I didn't think it was right.

After the game, many of us were gathered together outside the gym when my wife joked with me about getting the technical. I snapped and spoke to her in a hateful way. As you can imagine, there was dead silence from the folks standing with us.

That night, I had come with my friend Paul, one of the key men in my circle of leaders. Unexpectedly, as I sat silently in the car going home, the Holy Spirit showed me how wrong I was and how my behavior was inappropriate. That night, I told Paul that if I ever did that again, he had my permission to call me on it.

A month or so later (January), my phone rang at 1:30 a.m. in the morning. It was Paul. He said that he had to talk to me. I assured him that we could talk tomorrow. All I heard was "No...now!" And click!

Twenty minutes later, Paul arrived at my home. He got out of his truck and walked directly to me, weeping. I had no idea what had happened.

He told me that he was sorry, and that he wanted me to forgive him.

He said, "Do you remember what happened after the basketball game when you received a technical foul?"

I said, "Yes, I remember."

"Well, yesterday, you asked if we were going to meet today as we had planned, and I said NO. Well, I lied. I just didn't want to go. Then the Lord reminded me of our conversation in the truck. At that point, I realized that I, too, needed to apologize and ask for forgiveness. For that reason, I want to say, if I ever do something like that again, you have the right to call me on it. This is how important our relationship is to me."

It was the combination of *truth, relationship,* and the work of the *Holy Spirit* that made the difference. Now, twenty years later, our relationship is stronger than ever, and God is using Paul in powerful ways to spread the gospel message and what it means to follow Jesus.

PRAY, PRAY, PRAY

It is not hard to notice what was important to Jesus as He lived on earth. And it is not a surprise that it caught the attention of the disciples. Of all the things that Jesus did in their presence, which included speaking and performing miracles, it was His daily commitment to prayer that stood out.

It is even more incredible to read that this was the one thing the disciples asked Jesus to teach them. They asked Him because this was a priority in His life, and clearly, they assumed that it should be important for them as well. The writers of the New Testament affirm the importance of prayer too!

Paul the apostle completes his letter to the believers in Philippi with this appeal to the power of prayer:

> Do not be anxious about anything, but in everything by prayer and supplication with thanksgiving let your requests be made known to God. And the peace of God, which surpasses all understanding, will guard your hearts and your minds in Christ Jesus. (Phil. 4:6)

Apparently, Paul was one to practice the discipline of prayer too and was eager to pass its importance unto others.

> What you have learned and received and heard
> and seen in me, practice these things, and the
> God of peace will be with you. (Phil. 4:9)

The work of leading faithful men would include much more than passing on the teachings he had heard from Paul. It would be filled with times when the most important thing one could do is to pray. Leading the church in Ephesus would be a challenging task, but with the power of personal and corporate prayer, nothing could keep them from fulfilling their ministry (2 Tim. 4:5).

THE MESSAGE IS CLEAR

It is hard to miss the emphasis of Paul's letter to Timothy. He was to pass these things unto men who would continue the work of the church. He was to put these things before the brothers (1 Tim. 4:6) and command and teach these things (1 Tim. 4:11). He was to practice and immerse himself in this work (1 Tim. 4:15) and keep a watch on his progress. This was so important for him to do as he led a group of faithful men to do the same. By so doing, he would save both himself and his hearers (1 Tim. 4:16).

The challenge before us is to do the same. Who are our faithful men into whom we are passing on the faith? If we are not following this command, why? And if we see this as the work we need to be doing, when will we get started? Let's pray and hope that the church will find the missing piece before it's too late.

CHAPTER 9

THE BARE NECESSITIES

Man will occasionally stumble over the truth,
but most of the time he will pick himself up and continue on.

—Winston Churchill

Let's have faith that right makes might;
and in that faith let us, to the end, dare to
do our duty as we understand it.

—Abraham Lincoln

I grew up in a family where it was a common thing to hear my dad singing what we affectionately called *ditties*. The best way I know to describe a ditty is to say it's a song made up about a dog, a cat, a son or daughter, a grandchild, and *maybe even a mate*. They are silly and meant to be sung.

It's funny how much these songs stick in your mind. I also know where my dad got them from as I remember sitting on my grandfather's lap (his dad) and having him sing his own version of the Thumpytom song[78] to me. In case you are wondering, I have been

---

[78.] Thumpytom was a play on my first name (Thomas), which happened to be the same as my dad.

known to shout out a number of my own ditties and have seen my own boys take up the habit as well. It would be hard for our family to imagine it being any other way.

You may not be prone to do this, but I am quite certain that your view of life has been shaped by the way your family taught you to *think* and *behave.* It's possible that *your* parents were into the details, while others like to focus on the big picture. Both approaches to life have value and cannot be neglected.

It is understandable that people will typically prefer one way or another. The question at hand is whether or not it is important that we see both the details and the big picture. Most of us can remember describing someone who "can't see the forest for the trees," and equally true is the fact that we know people who are always buried in the details and aren't necessarily concerned about the end goal.

Jesus was concerned about both, and we see this in play in His final words to His disciples:

> Go therefore and make disciples of a nations, baptizing them in the name of the Father and of the Son ad of the Holy Spirit, teaching them to observe all that I have commanded you. (Matt. 28:16–20)

Notice the juxtaposition between the *details* of disciple-making versus the *big picture view.* The original disciples were to go and make disciples of all nations (big picture), but there was no mention of the fact that first they needed to see people believe in their heart and confess with their mouth (details) that Jesus is Lord in order to be saved (Rom. 10:10–13). They were to baptize them in the name of the Father, Son, and Holy Spirit (details) and teach them to observe *all* (big picture) that Jesus had commanded them.

Jesus understood the necessity of knowing your goal *and* being aware of what it would take to reach your goal.

> For which of you, desiring to build a tower, does not first sit down and count the cost, whether he has enough to complete it? Otherwise, when he has

laid a foundation and is not able to finish, all who see it begin to mock him, saying, "This man began to build and was not able to finish." Or what king, going out to encounter another king in war, will not sit down first and deliberate whether he is able with ten thousand to meet him who comes against him with twenty thousand? And if not, while the other is yet a great way off, he sends a delegation and asks for terms of peace, so therefore, any one of you who does not renounce all that he has cannot be my disciple. (Luke 14:28–33)

Anyone who desires to be a disciple must know what it will take to reach such an important goal. In the same way, any church body that seeks to become a disciple-making church must realize that it can't be *business as usual.* The traditional approach to life in the church today must drastically change from an informational model to a *transformational* model if we are to fulfill Jesus's command of making disciples.

NOT SO "PITCHER" PERFECT

It is very tempting to think of disciple-making merely as a transfer of information from one person to another, a fact that is reinforced every time one walks into a Christian bookstore and is confronted by a title that claims, "Ten Easy Steps to Making Disciples." If it were only that simple, one would expect an incredible harvest of results, but the truth is that making disciples is not accomplished in three, five, or even ten easy steps but through the sharing of one life with another over time about knowing Christ and what it means to serve Him for the rest of your life.

We see this in the words of Paul as he spoke about his relationship with the believers in Thessalonica:

So being, affectionately desirous of you, we were ready to share with you not only the gospel of

God but also our own selves, because you had become very dear to us. (1 Thess. 2:8)

It is almost certain that this was the view held by Timothy as well. One cannot imagine spending so much time with Paul on his trips and never getting a sense of how Paul related to the believers in the churches. These words make that clear:

> For you know how, like a father with his children, we exhorted each one of you and encouraged you and charged you to walk in a manner worthy of God, who calls you into his own kingdom and glory. (1 Thess. 2:12)

Paul's love and concern for the believers in Thessalonica was further demonstrated when he sent Timothy back to *establish and exhort* (details) them in their faith (1 Thess. 3:2). It is in Paul's response to Timothy's encouraging report on his trip to Thessalonica that we see his ultimate goal for the saints in the church (big picture).

> Now may our God and Father himself, and our Lord Jesus Christ direct our way to you, and may the Lord make you increase and abound in love for one another and for all, as we do for you, so that before our God and Father, at the coming of our Lord Jesus with all his saints (1 Thess. 3:11–13).

As Timothy assumed the role, passing on the faith to his *faithful men* (2 Tim. 2:1–2), one would expect to hear many of the same thoughts and see many of the same behaviors he saw in the life of Paul, and I, for one, wonder what that might look like.

YOU'RE NEXT

No one knows for certain when Timothy became a believer. It is possible that it happened during Paul's first trip to the cities of Lystra and Derbe (Acts 14:6–7). He obviously recognized in Timothy the potential to be a faithful servant of the Lord, which prompted him to ask him to join him on his missionary journeys (Acts 16:3).

Now, years later, Paul asked him to take on the major responsibility of guiding the local church in Ephesus by leading a group of *faithful men* to not only *possess the faith but pass it on.* With the big picture in mind, a closer look is demanded to see the details that were required of Timothy as he leads these men.

THE BARE NECESSITIES

Charged with this responsibility, Timothy must go back into the recesses of his mind and collect his thoughts about what will be needed to achieve Paul's mandate. With so many running through his mind, a few began to rise to the surface as the *bare necessities.* Like water and food for a person stranded on a deserted island, Paul revealed a few things that absolutely must be part of Timothy's attempt to bring the faithful men to full obedience. Even a cursory read of Paul's two letters to Timothy will reveal that certain commitments were critical to their health and success.

A HOT PURSUIT

It's been years, but I can still remember the feeling of being proud that my dad had been asked to preach the baccalaureate message for my graduation from Bible college. Dad had been a pastor and teacher for many years and was well-qualified for this task; nevertheless, I was thrilled that he was asked. More than this, I can recall with clarity the title of his message: "The Weakest Part of the Strongest Man." In case you didn't get it from the title, the message was about the life of Samson.

As students, we were challenged with the idea that every day becomes an opportunity for us to squander the good we have accomplished, or we could build upon the solid foundation we have begun to build. We could graduate with honors and land a great job only to see it fall flat due to a thing we call a lack of *character*.[79]

Character is an important piece when it comes to understanding the nature of Christ. The writer to Hebrews makes it clear in his opening thoughts that Jesus was "the radiance of the glory of God, and the exact imprint of his nature" (χαρακτηρ [Heb.1:3]). Here, Jesus is said to have the same *character* as God the Father. Once, while the disciples were with Jesus, Phillip asked Him to show them the Father; and if He did that, everything would be great. Jesus's response is quite revealing: "Have I been with you so long, and you still do not know me, Phillip? Whoever has seen me has seen the Father. How can you say, Show us the Father? Do you not believe that I am in the Father and the Father is in me? (John 14:9-10)"

The character of Jesus is the primary ingredient in His ability to shake up the world around Him. He was unique even though He was known as a simple carpenter's son. For this reason, we must give attention to the development of our character. We must pursue those things that will shape our lives into the people God can use to change our world for Christ. In the midst of all that was going on in Ephesus and in light of the charge he was to give to Timothy, Paul knew that he must make this a priority.

> Pursue righteousness, godliness, faith, love, steadfastness, gentleness. Fight the good fight of faith. Take hold of the eternal life to which you were called and about which you made the good confession in the presence of many witnesses. (1 Tim. 6:11–12)

History will show that many a leader, and even pastors, have failed to do what God called them to do due to a failure in the development of their character. Like Demas, who abandoned Paul because he loved the world more (2 Tim. 4:10), Timothy's faithful men must

---

79. The mental and moral qualities distinctive to an individual, or as a verb, it means to "inscribe" or "engrave" (Heb. 1:3).

be aware of the temptation to forget the importance of building a foundation in their lives of godly character.

Without question, this is one of the primary reasons that Paul was attracted to Timothy. He described him as one who had a *genuine or sincere* faith (ανυποκριτου)[80] (2 Tim. 1:5). No wonder Paul asked him to confront the false teachers in Ephesus. He was trustworthy and capable to do this work. Only now, he needed help in keeping it going since he was leaving (2 Tim. 4:9). If only he had some faithful men to help him who were defined by godly character traits.

SOUND DOCTRINE

For the first time, the words of Paul sent to Timothy in his final letter grabbed my attention like never before. My focus, as it is for most, if not all of us, has been on the written text, but then it hit me. The Scripture that Paul is describing as "God-breathed" is in reference to the written text of the Old Testament. This is the Word that is "profitable for teaching, for reproof, for correction, and for training in righteousness, that the man of God may be complete, equipped for every good work" (2 Tim. 3:16–17).

Today, it is not uncommon for believers to possess many written copies of the Bible, but the everyday person in the first century only heard the Scriptures read in the synagogue. Because of this, statements like "continue in what you have heard and firmly believed" (2 Tim. 3:14) and "what you have heard from me in the presence of many witnesses entrust to faithful men" (2 Tim. 2:2) give us insight into how the truth was *presented, discussed, accepted,* and *passed on to others.*

This meant that Timothy had three primary sources of truth: (1) the Old Testament Scriptures, (2) the truth of the gospel in his own life and the essence of the gospel revealed by Paul and others (1 Tim. 1:12–7), and (3) the written letters of Paul to him, explaining

---

80. Timothy is described by Paul as having an ανυποκριτου faith, which means that he did not wear a mask.

the life of the believer and the church (1 and 2 Tim.). Once grasped, it was Timothy's charge to "Preach the Word, be ready in season and out of season: reprove, rebuke, and exhort, with complete patience and teaching. For the time is coming when people will not endure **sound teaching** but having itching ears to hear they will accumulate for themselves teachers to suit their own passions and will turn away from listening to the truth and wander off into myths" (2 Tim. 4:2–4).

SMALL GROUP 101

How many "faithful men" made up Timothy's first group? I don't know for sure, but it probably functioned quite differently than our modern-day understanding of a small group. They were not there simply to talk *about* a topic (not a passage, unless it was from the Old Testament) but rather to interact with each other for the purpose of determining the truth and discovering how they were to live in light of it. Timothy would provide the topic or issue and let the Holy Spirit guide them as they interacted. They weren't concerned about asking what it means to you but instead, "what do you believe God meant by this or that?"

In 1897, Charles Sheldon wrote what is now considered a classic book entitled *In His Steps*. The book was written during the Social Gospel Movement but began as stories which turned into sermons for his church. His stories begin in an upscale church when a homeless man walks in during a service and confronts the church's hypocrisy. His fictional book asks a very important question: What would Jesus do? However, when one thinks about sound doctrine, one must not guess what Jesus would do but instead seek to know WDJD (What Did Jesus Do). Once discovered, followers of Christ can know exactly what they need to do.

Each time Timothy met with the faithful men, they would spend considerable time wrestling with questions like:

- What is the essence of the gospel (2 Tim. 4:17)?
- How do we respond to false teachers (1 Tim. 1:3–8)?

- How do I respond to suffering (2 Tim. 2:8–13)?
- How do we rightly handle the Word of truth (2 Tim. 2:14–16)?
- How do I pursue righteousness (1 Tim. 6:11–16)?
- What is the proper role of prayer in my life, in my church (1 Tim. 2:1–8)?
- How do I keep a close watch on myself (1 Tim. 4:11–16)?
- How do I keep a closer watch on my teaching (1 Tim. 4:11–16)?
- What does it mean to do good works and how do they relate to the gospel (1 Timothy 1:12–17)?

These questions and many more are to be talked about, discussed, prayed about, studied, and saturated with the leading of the Holy Spirit (Eph. 6:17, 2 Tim. 2:7). Based upon this practice in the early church, one must ask whether or not we should be doing the same thing today. If so, what would that look like in today's culture? How does a pastor begin to make certain that the truths of the Scriptures are passed on to the next generation?

BACK TO SQUARE ONE

Back to square one is an idiomatic expression that has to do with starting over after some attempt to accomplish a specific task or goal has failed to produce the desired results. One is hard-pressed to say that the church has been successful at fulfilling the mandate given by Jesus to his disciples (Matt. 28:16–20) and the failure of the local church to carry on the charge given to Timothy (2 Tim. 2:1–2).

A modern-day application of Timothy's approach to living out the mandate given by Paul must be applied with caution. There is a great temptation to become verbose as we describe the process of making disciples. It might be wise to consider Occam's razor as we proceed.

Occam's razor is the problem-solving principle that states that "Entities should not be multiplied without necessity." The idea is attributed to English Franciscan William of Ockham (c. 1287–

1347). It is sometimes paraphrased by a statement like "the simplest solution is most likely the right one."

I am quite certain that as the false teachers caught wind of what Timothy was doing, there were many suggestions as to how truth is determined and how to pass it on. Paul's strategy was indeed simple: Command and teach these things. Let no one despise you for your youth, but set the believers an example in speech, in conduct, in love, in faith, in purity. Until I come, devote yourself to the public, reading of Scripture, to exhortation, to teaching. Do not neglect the gift you have, which was given you by prophecy when the council of elders laid their hands on you. Practice these things, immerse yourself in them so that all may see your progress. Keep a close watch on yourself and on the teaching. Persist in this, for by so doing, you will save both yourself and your hearers (1 Tim. 4:11–16).

If we apply the principle of Occam's razor to the ministry of the local church today, it might look like the following—simple, clear, and persistent:

(PRAY) Prayerfully select a few men/women who are willing to join you in this journey.

(PICK) Clearly communicate the ultimate goal of your relationship.

(PREPARE) Identify the subjects, issues, and behaviors to be discussed and determined.

(PRACTICE) Commit to obedience in whatever is determined to be truth.

(PRESENT) Clarify the expectations to all who are involved.

(POSE) Regularly seek God's thoughts on how you are doing at every turn.

Through a pursuit of righteousness, and an understanding of sound doctrine, Timothy is ready to use the most practical element available to him for the passing on of truth to his faithful men: the power of relationships.

RELATIONAL DISCIPLESHIP

For some, it may seem like an irrelevant question to ask why Jesus picked twelve men to join Him as His disciples *in training*, but the more one reads the biblical account, it would seem that there are some not-so-obvious reasons for his approach that are worth consideration.

First to be carefully weighed in terms of its importance is the amount of time before Jesus actually called the twelve men to become His disciples. According to the work of Dann Spader, Jesus knew the men before He called them.

> Without a chronological understanding of Jesus' life, few realize that Mark 1:17, where Jesus tells His disciples "follow me and I will make you fishers of men," is not His first connection with these disciples. At that point, they had been with Jesus for at least eighteen months and now he is calling them to a new level of involvement and development. When Jesus chose the twelve apostles (Luke 6:12–16), He had been investing in them for two and a half years. Understanding the chronology of Jesus' life helps us to understand how He developed His disciples.

Spader writes that John 3:22 tells us that Jesus "spent time with his disciples." The Greek word translated "spent time with" here is *diatribo* (diatribo). It means "getting under the skin of." Jesus gave His disciples time to get to know Him and took time to invest in them.[81] It even appears that prior to calling the Twelve, Jesus focused His attention on five men (Peter, Andrew, James, John, and Matthew) before calling all of them to join Him (Matt. 4:18–22, 9:9).

[81.] Dann Spader, *4 Chair Disicipling: Growing a Movement of Disciple-Makers* (Moody Publishers, Chicago, IL, 2014), pg. 14–16.

In his classic work *The Training of the Twelve*, A. B. Bruce suggests that there was a reason Jesus eventually picked twelve men.

> It is probable that the selection of a limited number to be his close and constant companions had become a necessity to Christ, in consequence of His very success in gaining disciples. His followers, we imagine, had grown so numerous as to be an encumbrance and an impediment to his movements, especially in the long journeys which mark the latter part of His ministry. It was impossible that all who believed could continue henceforth to follow Him, in the literal sense, whithersoever He might go: the greater number could now only be occasional followers. But it was His wish that certain men should be with Him at all times and in all places-His traveling companions in all His wanderings, witnessing all His work, and ministering to His daily needs.[82]

This idea is captured succinctly by Mark in his gospel, chapter 3 verses 13 to 15:

> And he went up on the mountain and called to him those he desired, and they came to him. And he appointed twelve (whom he also named apostles) **so that they might be with him** and he might send them out to preach and have authority to cast out demons.

[82.] A. B. Bruce, *The Training of the Twelve,* (Kregel Publications, Grand Rapids, MI 49501) pg. 29–30.

A MOTLEY CREW

When one considers the task that Jesus was calling these men to be a part of, one might second-guess His choices. Could they work together and carry out the work of preaching the gospel as Jesus desired? There are those who might argue that the group should be *homogeneous*.[83] They should all be the same, especially in the way they think and act. The shocker is the fact that Jesus's selections for being part of the twelve disciples could not be more heterogeneous.[84] They are very different and do not think or act the same. A brief overview of the twelve disciples shows us just how different they were.

- **Thomas**—Most people know Thomas due to his encounter with Jesus, where he doubted that Jesus had really risen from the dead (John 20:24–29). Thomas was not present for some reason when Jesus first appeared to the Twelve following the resurrection (John 20:19–23). His reaction was like, "Yeah, right!" However, it was true; Jesus had risen from the dead. Thomas would not believe unless he could see it for himself and touch him with his own hands. *I wonder if Thomas ever doubted anything else while he spent time with Jesus.*
- **Simon the Zealot**—It is possible that Simon was a member of one of the revolutionary factions who, after the collapse of resistance to the Romans in Galilee, inspired the fanatical stand in *Jerusalem, which led to its destruction in AD 70.[85] Or it could simply be a reference to equivalents for "zealous defender, enthusiast, one eager to acquire, fanatic" (from root words, meaning "burn with zeal, or

---

83. *Homogeneous*, meaning "consisting of parts all of the same kind."
84. *Heterogeneous*, meaning "diverse in character or content."
85. Cross, F. L., Livingstone, E. A. (Eds.). (2005). In *The Oxford dictionary of the Christian Church* (3rd ed. rev., p. 1792). Oxford; New York: Oxford University Press.

jealousy; desire eagerly" [Exod. 34:14, 2 Macc. 4:2]).[86] *Do you think Simon might have gotten quite excited about some of the things going on in reaction to Jesus? At what point did he become zealous for Jesus and the things of the kingdom of God?*

- **Andrew**—We know that Andrew was Simon Peter's brother (Matt. 10:2). But we also know that Andrew was somewhat observant as he was the disciple who noticed the young boy in the midst of a great crowd of people who had five barley loaves and two fish (John 6:8–9). He offered that to Jesus, not knowing what Jesus would do. *Do you think Andrew noticed other things throughout their life together that Jesus would multiply for the greater good?*

- **Matthew**—One day, Jesus stopped by a tax booth and called Matthew to follow Him (Matt. 9:9). One can only imagine the ripple effect among the first four disciples when Jesus asked Matthew the tax collector to join them (Matt. 4:18–22). Jesus loved tax collectors but hated the corruption commonly found among them. *Do you think Matthew was tempted to cut corners to gain an advantage with others, or is it likely that Matthew once confronted with Christ took on the attitude of the tax collector we read about in Luke 10:8–14?*

- **James and John**—Known as the "sons of thunder," a name given to them by Jesus Himself (Mark 3:17). Why would Jesus call them by this name? Could it be because of their reaction to other situations (Mark 9:54)? *Given all the situations encountered by Jesus and His disciples, can you imagine James and John reacting this way on other occasions?*

- **Judas**—The one who betrayed Jesus for money. This was not the first time money was on Judas's mind. He is the disciple who criticized the waste of an expensive ointment to wash the feet of Jesus and suggest that it could add to the fund for the apostles, which would certainly mean more

---

[86]. Elwell, W. A., & Beitzel, B. J. (1988). Zealot. In *Baker encyclopedia of the Bible* (vol. 2, p. 2179). Grand Rapids, MI: Baker Book House.

money available to him (John 12:3–5). He even suggests that the money could be given to the poor, which would appear to be pure deceit on his part. Interestingly, immediately after this event, Judas went to the chief priests to betray the Lord (Matthew 26:14–16). *Do you think this type of behavior had reared its head before?* Being fully aware of Judas's heart condition, it is amazing that Jesus washed his feet in the upper room.

- **Phillip**—the inquisitive one. He wanted to know the answers to his deepest spiritual questions like, "Show us the Father and it is enough for us" (John 14:8). I can only imagine how many times Phillip wanted to ask questions about the things Jesus talked about or the things He was doing. *It would be surprising to find out that he didn't have questions on many occasions in the life he shared with Jesus.*
- **Peter**—Known for his "jump to the gun" approach to most everything, Peter is easily the best known of the twelve disciples. He is bold and *impetuous* in all his actions. From the beginning, he was in the process of becoming all that Jesus knew he would be. From the name of Simon, to the nickname of Cephas or Peter (Rock), we see the prophecy of Jesus about him become true. In the end, he became one of the pillars of the early church (Acts 2:14–41). *The conversations among Jesus and His eleven other disciples were no doubt enlivened by the personality and presence of Peter.*

Add to this group of people *Nathaniel, James the Greater, Judas Thaddeus,* and *James the Lesser* and you have quite the group. Even though we know virtually nothing about this remaining group of disciples, their presence shows us the importance of everyone when it comes to carrying out the work of Jesus. Everyone is needed.

The approach taken by Jesus in putting together His group of disciples gives us good insight into our work of making disciples and passing on the faith. First, it is *a strategic process of multiplying disciples.* We are not simply *adding* disciples. It is too slow and suggests the possibility that only a few or maybe even just a pastor or leader is doing it. We are called to multiply disciples, and this argues for a group of people or an entire church living out this mandate of making disciples.

Like Jesus, we must spend time investing in a few people in whom we believe are interested in pursuing Christ at a deeper and different level. At the proper time, we must invite them to join us in the journey of becoming a fully developed follower of Christ. It may be a unique and even peculiar gathering of people, as seen in the makeup of the original disciples, but that's okay. All they did, was "turn the world upside down."

Secondly, it is *an intentionally relational process.* We are extending an invitation to people to join us on a life-changing journey. It is much more than a transfer of information. Rather, it is a *transformational experience* of believing the truth about Christ and His Word and together seeking to live out the implications of that truth in everything we do.

Finally, it is *a perpetual process.* It is not terminal in its focus. We are not aiming at getting done in three to five years. It is ongoing until Christ returns. This means that we are making disciples and equipping the saints so they can do the same with others and keep it going. Regardless of when or why they ask what we are doing in and through the church, the answer is always the same: *we are making disciples who make disciples.*

GET TO WORK

Timothy has received the charge from Paul to pass on the faith through faithful men. Now, he must pick those he wants to spend time with. They are to be *faithful, available, and teachable.*

- *Faithful*—They must be people of faith not only in Christ but people who are trustworthy and dependable.
- *Available*—Becoming a fully developed disciple of Jesus is not a part-time job. You are not trying to fit Jesus into your schedule.

- *Teachable*—You are eager to be taught and helped to apply the sound doctrine of the Scriptures.

MODERN-DAY MINISTRY

It is time for the present-day pastor and, on a broader scale, the church to rethink what it means to be the church. It is time to reconsider our *priorities* for ministry. We cannot be satisfied with the upkeep of our facilities, the planning and implementation of our programs, how much money we have in our bank account, and even our level of outreach. It is time to return to the biblical standard of what it means to be a disciple-making person.

CHAPTER 10

A RECIPE FOR SUCCESS

Success is where preparation and opportunity meet.

—Bobby Unser

The resurrection of Jesus was now becoming a reality in the minds of believers. For forty days, Jesus appeared to many people, giving proof that He was alive. This may not sound like a long time, but when you are eager to know what's next, it probably seemed like forever. One can only imagine the questions the disciples had for Jesus during this time, but it's clear that Jesus had one particular thing on His mind: *the kingdom of God* (Acts 1:3).

During His short time on earth, Jesus spoke of the kingdom of God by connecting Himself with the message that He and His followers proclaimed. Luke records a time when Jesus sent out seventy-two people to preach the gospel and represent His kingdom. In this passage, one can see an inseparable connection between Jesus and the message of the kingdom of God.

> Whenever you enter a town and they receive you, eat what is set before you. Heal the sick in it and say to them, "The Kingdom of God has come near to you." But whenever you enter a town and they do but receive you, go into its streets and

say, "Even the dust of your tow that clings to our feet we wipe off against you. Nevertheless, know this, that the Kingdom of God has come near." (Luke 10:9–12)

This was a powerful example of the way Jesus that put into place His strategy of bringing the message of the kingdom to a lost world. He chose people to represent Him and His message to a lost world. At that time, Jesus was still on earth, but now He is leaving this world to return to His Father (John 17). For this reason, He established the church to carry out His plan.

THE QUESTION

One is tempted to go immediately to Acts 2:42–47 for a picture of the early church following the return of Christ to His Father, but the church began in that first gathering of His disciples when they asked, "Lord, will you at this time restore the kingdom to Israel" (Acts 1:6)?

Despite the fact that the disciples were still stuck on the idea of a *national kingdom*, Jesus patiently prepared them for the time when they would become His church.

A RECIPE FOR SUCCESS

After years of doing life together, one would think that the disciples were fully equipped to carry out their master's mandate to make disciples. They had followed Jesus for over three years and listened to Him teach about the kingdom of God. They were there when He healed the sick and cast out demons (Matt. 9:32–34). They participated in carrying out many of His miracles such as the feeding of the five thousand with a few loaves and fishes (Matt. 14:13–21), the raising of the dead (John 11:38–44), and walking on water (Matt. 14:22–33).

According to the Apostle John, Jesus trained them and equipped them to be disciple-makers. He writes at the beginning of his priestly prayer in John 17. He said, "I have glorified you on earth, having accomplished the work that you gave me to do." This statement refers to His work with the disciples and was made prior to His death, burial, and resurrection. As He was preparing to return to His Father, He told them to wait for one more thing: *the person and power of the Holy Spirit* (Acts 1:8). By receiving the Holy Spirit, they would become his effective "witnesses in *Jerusalem, Judea, Samaria and to the end of the earth.*" So they waited!

They waited until God honored His prophetic word spoken by Joel:

> And it shall come to pass afterward, that I will pour out my Spirit on all flesh, and your sons and your daughters shall prophesy, and your young men shall see visions, and your old men shall dream dreams; even on my male servants and female servants in those days I will pour out my Spirit, and they shall prophesy. (Joel 2:28–29)

According to Peter, the disciples were recipients of this promise:

> This Jesus God raised up, and of that we are all witnesses. Being therefore exalted at the right hand of God and having received from the Father the promise of the Holy Spirit, he has poured out this that you yourselves are seeing and hearing. (Acts 2:32–33)

A SOLID FOUNDATION

When one thinks of the church today, it may not cross one's mind that this was the beginning of the *church* as we know it. Questions like, "What was it that made it possible for the early church to flourish in the first century culture?" and "What did the church do to establish itself and pave the way for its exponential growth?"

The words of the Apostle Peter as he responded to the questions of the early believers help us understand the beginning of the church. People wondered what they were supposed to do with the good news of Jesus. How were they supposed to live? Luke gave us insight into the strategy that the young church must follow. After reminding them of the promised Holy Spirit (Acts 2:38), Peter exhorted them with these words: "Save yourselves from this crooked generation" (Acts 2:40).

Peter used an interesting word to describe the number one goal of the new church. They were to "save" themselves from all that sought to stop them. While this word might include a reference to their salvation in Christ, it also includes keeping away from those things that seek to destroy and keep it from doing what God called it to do. The Apostle Paul opted to use the same word as Luke did. It provides a deeper understanding of why Peter used the word *save* (swzw) to make his exhortation to the early church.

The church in Ephesus was experiencing its own problems. False teachers were influencing the church, especially the women in it. The influence of the false teachers was reaching into the home and moving into the church. Paul's words to Timothy about the women may seem harsh at first look, but on a closer examination, it all makes sense.

The word *save* (σωζω) is often translated and understood to mean "kept safe." One of the primary reasons Paul uses this word is for the fact that the women of Ephesus had forgotten or abandoned their God-ordained role in the family. They were to be a helper to their husbands. They were not to usurp their role as the head of the family. Because Eve sinned first (1 Tim. 2:14), all women would be reminded of their proper role in the family through childbearing (1 Tim. 2:15). In Ephesus, the women were forgetting God's promise to Eve.

A simple remedy was offered by Paul: "Yet she will be **saved through childbearing**—if they continue in faith and love and holiness, with self-control (1 Tim. 2:15). By remembering God's words to Eve every time, they experienced the pain of childbirth. A woman could keep her family safe and prevent the destruction of the family and prevent it from being infected with the beliefs and ideas of the false teachers. In the same way, the early church could keep itself safe from a crooked generation by adhering to the words of Peter.

My personal experience with childbirth made it clear to me that in order to receive joy, one almost certainly will go through pain.

ICE CHIPS, SCREAMS, AND A BABY

I guess that I am like most expecting fathers when they are awaiting their firstborn child. Thirty-nine years ago, we were awaiting the birth of our oldest son. It was early in the morning, and we were prepared as we could be. Lamaze classes were over, prayers had been made for health, and we were just waiting for it all to happen.

Just before it all took place, my wife asked if I would go and get her some ice chips, so off I went. Shortly before I made it back to the birthing room, I heard a blood-curdling scream that sounded something like this: "SAAAAAMMMMM!" Well, I hurried to the room, having spilled all of the ice chips, just in time to hear my wife ask, "Where did you go?"

We didn't have to wait too long before our son arrived but not prior to a lot of pain. I must admit that while men think that they are tough and can handle pain well, *they haven't given birth.* Yet an amazing thing happened after it was over. There was nothing but joy as we met our son for the first time. Shelly helped our family grow and remain healthy by doing the thing only she could do: give birth. It was painful but worth it in the end.

Just as the church in Ephesus could be sabotaged by the unwillingness to keep themselves safe from the influence of the false teachers, the early church was also in danger if they couldn't keep safe from the influence of the crooked generation surrounding them.

In Paul's final letter to Timothy, he warned him of the potential dangers posed by the society surrounding the church:

> But understand this, that in the last days there will come times of difficulty. For people will be lovers of self, lovers of money, proud, arrogant,

abusive, disobedient to their parents, ungrate-
ful, unholy, heartless, unappeasable, slanderous,
without self-control, brutal, not loving good,
treacherous, reckless, swollen with conceit, lovers
of pleasure rather than lovers of God, having the
appearance of godliness, but denying its power.
Avoid such people. (2 Tim. 3:1–5)

It is more than likely that the lifestyle assumed by the early
church was suggested by Peter and revealed in the words of Acts
2:42–47.

How do you keep safe? What must the church do to make certain that they are safe and able to do what God called them to do?
They must be devoted to at least four primary functions that would
keep them safe from the influence of the world and bring the gospel
to those who came into contact with the church.

FULLY DEVOTED

They were devoted to the *apostle's teaching* (Acts 2:42). Luke
chose a word that (for many) might be unexpected. One would think
that they would focus on the *kerygma* (or gospel message) since so
many had recently believed and become part of the church. While
this makes sense, it is not the focus of devotion for the church.

The apostle's teaching, known as Didache (διδαχη), referred
to the many things that the Lord had taught His disciples that were
passed down to people like Paul and Peter. Building on the commission given by Jesus to His original disciples, the early church was fully
committed to obeying everything that they were commanded to do
(Matt. 28:16–20). These became the plumb line for knowing what
to do and how to do it.

Armed with truth and purpose, the church devoted themselves
to the *fellowship, to the breaking of bread* (Acts 2:42), and to *the
prayers.* During this time of persecution and evil, the church perse-
vered in the things most precious to God's family: *righteousness, relationships, remembrance,* and *requests.* They were devoted to knowing

the ways of God, the importance of staying connected in the body of Christ, the remembering of all that God has done for the believer and the sharing of His blessings, and the constant practice of the church's dependence on God for all that is needed through prayer (1 Tim. 2:1–6).

THOSE WHO WERE BEING SAVED

Their devotion was all done for a very specific purpose. Their life together, while such a beautiful and powerful picture of God's presence, was all for one reason. *Ironically,* the church was created to reach the "crooked generation" that they were told to avoid.

This is why Acts 2:47 is so important—then and now! Luke wrote: "And the Lord added to their number day by day those who were being saved." For years, I have read this verse and wondered how this happened. How was it that this group of people were able to make such an amazing impact on their world? Why was the church so effective? Perhaps these are the wrong questions. Is it possible that the reason that the church grew so much in its beginning is simpler than we might think?

I have always been impressed with the fact that on the day of Pentecost, over three thousand people came to faith and were incorporated into the life of the church. This made me laugh as I thought about the church of today when having ten people in a new believers' class might be a challenge. What about three thousand?

This alone makes it clear that the early church knew what to do with them as they were incorporated into the life of the body. It is quite obvious as well that the early church did not simply spend time together. They did not study for the sake of studying. They did not pray repetitious prayers that have nothing to do with the kingdom of God. They did not eat meals together and fellowship with each other on a regular basis just because that's what they did on Wednesday nights. No, it was much, much more!

When the early church dispersed into their community, they brought their knowledge of God's Word and ways. They brought their ability to build relationships into every encounter that they had with people. They invited people to join them for meals in their homes, which gave them the opportunity to see families being led by Christ. And they prayed for their friend's salvation, their pagan leaders, and their ability to live quiet and godly lives (1 Tim. 2:2–3).

The early church understood the life of the body, and they understood their culture. They knew how to bring the ways of Christ into a pagan and crooked world. They were disciples in the purest sense.

DISCIPLE-MAKING

The pattern of life for the disciple begun in the early church is the same instruction given to Timothy while serving the church in Ephesus (2 Tim. 2:1–2). They were to pass on the faith to others so that they could do the same. Given the condition of most local churches today, something went wrong.

A failure to "keep safe" from the pagan culture of our time and the absence of passing on the faith has led to a church that is anemic. As I have sought to describe in this book, the church must get back to living out the mandate of Christ in our own context and in our own time.

DIFFERENT TIME, SAME STROKES

Some will say that it's different today, and they are right. The twenty-first century is quite different from the first century; yet they are very much alike. Just as the first church prepared itself to bring the gospel to a world apart from Christ, so must the church of today do the same.

We cannot make the mistake that was made by the explorers *Meriwether Lewis* and *William Clark* in their attempt to travel across America to the shores of the Pacific Ocean. Their mistake was that they believed that the unexplored west was exactly the same (geographically) as the familiar east. We cannot assume that everything is the same and that there is no need for change.

In his insightful book *Canoeing the Mountains*, Tod Bolsinger takes a close look at the journey of Lewis and Clark, noting at least three necessary skills for them as they navigate their way.

- ***Understanding the Uncharted Territory.*** Lewis and Clark assumed that the geography of the east was the same in the west. Their calculation was faulty that they thought they could canoe all the way to the Pacific Ocean. But everything changed when they ran into mountain ranges. What would they do? They couldn't canoe the mountains.

  Their mistake helps us understand how important it is to *understand the uncharted territory* that you are facing. Today's church must not make the mistake of thinking that nothing has changed. Sin is sin, but the way that it is presented may look totally different. Knowing how to recognize the difference is a key skill needed in the church today.

- ***Leadership on the map is needed first.*** Lewis and Clark could not expect someone who is skilled in canoeing to be able to know how to climb the mammoth peaks that lay before them. They must be able to adapt to the change in environment in order to navigate through the territory.

  The inability to function properly on the map (in the church) can prohibit one from being able do what they are called to do in uncharted territory. Like men on Shackleton's ship, the people attempting to make the trip to the west coast had to be able to function in the right way when it gets tough.

  A believer that *lives by faith* on the map, must *live by faith* off the map. A person who claims to be a disciple on the map must be a disciple off the map.

- ***Adaptation is everything off the map.*** The ability to make it off the map is not only built on one's training and equipping on the map, it is the ability to adapt to anything they encounter.

  The church of today must be willing to meet people where they are and bring them to Jesus. We cannot expect those who do not believe in Christ to act like they believe. We cannot change our convictions about Christ and what is true, but we must move toward the lost in a way that gives us an opportunity to build a relationship that has the potential to lead them to faith in Christ.

THE CONTEMPORARY CHURCH

The world of today does not need the bells and whistles that we often think will impress them. They don't need a big facility or an amazing band to play music. The first disciples had none of these. What they need is a church full of people who love Christ so much that they are willing to get out of their comfort zone and enter the uncharted territory of their communities, workplaces, and places of leisure to show others what it means to have life in Christ.

CHAPTER 11

A BIBLICAL PLAN FOR
MAKING DISCIPLES

Go therefore and make Disciples.

—Matthew 28:18

After reading this book, it may still seem unclear as to what one is supposed to do with the information and ideas that have been shared. For that reason, this document was created in an effort to assist pastors and church leaders in their effort to become *disciple-making churches.*

Each part of this plan finds its support in the pages of this book. A revisit to the material in the book will be necessary along the way to ensure a good grasp of what is being proposed. To maximize the use of the book, and to benefit from this plan, you are encouraged to proceed slowly and carefully so as to not miss anything.

While this plan will be presented somewhat sequentially, one may choose to jump to a particular area of the plan that is most urgent for them, given the condition of their ministry. To gain the ultimate benefit from the plan, it is encouraged that you do this with your leaders in a group setting.

As you begin the process, it is wise to consider again the words of Dann Spader in his book (*4 Chair Discipling*), in which he argues that many Christians do not know or they forget that Jesus not only had a **message**, He also had a **method**. This plan is intended to highlight the method that Jesus and His followers used throughout the New Testament to make disciples and raise up leaders. This plan will build upon the belief that just as the first century church followed His plan, we too. We, who are in the twenty-first century, must do the same.

THE PLAN

A Strategic Prayer Focus

The early church devoted themselves to *the* prayers. As was argued previously, the Pentecost believers were devoted to more than simply praying (Acts 2:42–47). If we take a clue from the contemporary church, many of our prayers are inwardly focused. If we pray outside of our own needs, it is often limited to matters of health and needs that arise from things that happen in the life of the average person.

The fact that Luke used the definite article *the* in Acts 2:42 suggests that he had in mind much more than simply praying. He was thinking about certain types of prayers that would impact the overall health and ministry of the church body.

We could say that Paul told us to "pray without ceasing" (1 Thess. 5:17), but this does not give us clarity on the nature of the prayers. He also told Timothy to offer up prayers for those in authority (1 Tim. 2:1–7) so that believers could live a peaceful and quiet life. God does not want anything to prevent the hearing of the gospel and people getting saved.

INTO THE CLOSET

There is something about being in a leadership position that fuels our desire to be up front and in charge. However, the power that infuses a pastor or church leader comes first in private. He must be committed to starting his focused ministry in private.

Jesus provided a perfect example of the priority of prayer for His disciples. Much of His prayer time was spent alone. His practice of prayer was so noticeable that it is the one thing that His disciples asked Him to teach them (Luke 11:1). What might happen in the church if the pastor was as committed to prayer as Jesus?

Long before attempting to lead a church into a ministry that focuses on the making of disciples, the leaders of the church must commit themselves to prayer. Not a simple and short "help us make disciples" kind of prayer but a passionate pursuit of His direction as you go about making disciples. This will take time.

It is interesting to note that after all that Jesus had shown them through His commitment to prayer, the disciples couldn't stay awake to pray when He needed them the most (Luke 22:40–46). When we allow the schedules of our lives to wear us out so that we cannot pray, we must reevaluate the use of our time.

There is no magic formula on how long to pray. In reality, you never stop being a person of prayer. You do, however, pray long enough to know when God is giving you direction in your life and ministry. When a pastor reaches this point, it should be an opportunity to ask others to join him.

Many things don't happen in the life of a church for the simple reason that the pastor does it alone. He must build a team to go forward. A team that has the same convictions concerning what God is wanting them to build together. Prayer is a perfect setting for this to happen. I have often heard it said that God speaks the loudest when we pray. For Him to speak, we must pray.

A DIFFERENT MODEL

For as long as I can remember, every Wednesday night, our family went to church every Wednesday night for what was called prayer meeting. We would gather in the sanctuary (in our pews) and listen to the pastor tell us our prayer concerns, which almost always included those *private and unspoken requests.*

Every week, we would hear a litany of petitions that we were asked to pray for, and many weeks, they were the same. What if that all changed? What if we allowed the gathering of God's church to be led by the Holy Spirit? What might we see happen in our times of prayer?

Some have suggested that we use a guide such as the acronym ACTS (Adoration, Confession, Thanksgiving, and Supplication) to lead us through our times or prayer. This is fine, but what if this were happening as the Holy Spirit was moving upon the hearts of men and women as they gathered to pray?

Take a journey through a book like Psalms, and discover the natural flow of one who comes before the Lord in prayer! He is confident in God's provision, his trust is in the Lord, and he is constantly found begging for understanding of God's ways.

POSITION PRECEDES PETITION

When one thinks about the early church, the image of people sitting around in chairs or on benches as they participate in a prayer meeting seems foreign. True prayer events engage our mind, heart, and body. It was common for the people of God to **bow** before God as an act of worship.

> And Ezra opened the book I the sight of all the people, for he was above all the people, and as he opened it all the people stood. And Ezra blessed the Lord, the great God and all the people answered, "Amen, Amen," lifting up their hands. And they **bowed their heads and worshiped the Lord with their faces to the ground.** (Neh. 8:6)

Or to lay **prostrate** in His presence.

> While Ezra prayed and made confession, weeping and **casting himself down before the house of God** a very great assembly of men, women and children, gathered to him out of Israel, for the people wept bitterly. **(Ezra 10:1)**

In 1 Timothy (1 Tim. 2:8), Paul declared that he desired all men to **lift up holy hands without anger or quarreling** when they prayed, highlighting the importance of Christians coming before the Lord, having confessed their sins and walking in righteousness.

This passage emphasizes the fact that it is not only about coming together to pray but the condition of our lives when we come. As we set our ministries toward the mark of making disciples, let's make certain that we bring this matter before the Lord long before we start doing it.

A *Purposeful Plan for Preaching*

Prayer and preaching are twins in the work of the pastor. Not only does he need to preach, he needs to pray about what he preaches. Years ago, like others, I was told to put together a preaching plan for several months. For me, the problem with this approach was that it tempted me to put together a plan to preach on topics that sound good rather than a plan guided by the Holy Spirit.

So what does the pastor do to create a purposeful plan for preaching as he seeks to lead his church to make disciples? Preaching cannot be judged on the basis of whether it sounded good but rather on whether or not it is producing its desired results.

According to the writings of the Apostle Paul, the goal of preaching the Scriptures is clear:

> All Scripture is breathed out by God and **profitable for teaching, for reproof, for correction, and for training in righteousness, that the man of God may be complete, equipped for every good work.**

And,

> Preach the word, be ready in season and out of season; **reprove, rebuke, and exhort, with complete patience and teaching**. For the time

is coming when people will not endure sound teaching but having itching ears, they will accumulate for themselves teachers to suit their own passions and will turn away from listening to the truth and wander off into myths.

If we let *Scripture interpret Scripture* serve as the guiding principle in determining what we preach, then a "complete, for every good work" kind of man is one who is becoming what God wants all men to become, namely, *a fully devoted disciple of God* (Matt. 28:16–20).

We evaluate a text on its usefulness in helping our flock take a step forward in our journey to become disciples. To provide a consistent picture of the Bible's teaching, it is beneficial to preach through a book in an expositional manner, which allows us to address topics as they arise in the text. This approach gives the preacher an opportunity to address difficult topics with the purpose of shaping the mind and heart of a disciple without zeroing in on any person's need.

DOWNLOADING THE APP

In the first century, the expression "downloading the app" would have no meaning; but for us in the twenty-first century, it means a lot. This statement suggests the idea that in order for one to access the power of an idea or use of a tool, one must download it.

I have many applications (apps) on my phone that are there so that I can use them for their designed purpose. Preaching is not done simply to fill a time slot in worship service. The goal of preaching is the eventual transformation of those who preach and those who hear the preaching. As mentioned in the book, **"What DID Jesus do?"** rather than **"What would Jesus do?"** (**WWJD**) is to be our priority when preaching the Word. It is not a subjective question for the hearer who tries to imagine what Jesus would do. If the hearer does not know and understand the Scriptures and what is being taught, there is little chance that they will know what He did and what they must do.

I now realize that my preaching professors were right. Besides understanding the original intent of the text, the most important and often the most difficult aspect of biblical preaching for the pastor is the *application of the text and its meaning for today.*

Biblical preaching's goal is not only to present the truth of the text but also to guide the hearer in an appropriate application of the text to their life. With this in mind, we turn now to the third part of a biblical plan for making disciples: ***How are we to pass on these truths beyond preaching?***

A Practical Plan of Multiplication

Luke wrote that people were added to the church daily (Acts 2:47). As discussed in the book, it is clear that they knew what to do with them when they joined the church. Previous to this, three thousand new converts joined the church and were added to the church body (Acts 2:41), and it is evident that they knew what to do as seen in their devotion to the basics of life in the church (Acts 2:42).

History bears proof that the church continued to grow, but it was not by *addition.* Mere addition will not grow the church as Jesus intended it to grow. A brief illustration can describe the difference.

ADDITION MULTIPLICATION

1	1
2	2
3	4
4	8
5	16
6	32
7	64
8	128
9	256
10	512

It is exciting to see people come to the Lord in faith, but it is even more wonderful to see a group of people understand what it means to make disciples and find success in doing it. It is not likely that everyone who comes to faith will lead someone else to faith and nurture them into a fully developed disciple, but it IS POSSIBLE that many will grasp the gospel by faith and pass it on to another person.

> You then, my child, be strengthened by the grace that is in Christ Jesus and what you have heard from me in the presence of many witnesses **entrust** to faithful men who **will be able to teach others also.** (2 Tim. 2:1–2)

One should not forget that this is also the reason that Jesus selected twelve men to come to Him so they might be "**with**" Him (Mark 3:14), as well as the fact that not all twelve men made it to the end. Even Jesus did not have twelve men who believed Him and trusted Him completely.

Timothy took a few men (we don't know how many) and did the work to pass on the faith through, sharing with them all that he had learned from Paul and others. As evidenced through the New Testament, it worked.

A CURIOUS THOUGHT

This is where the prayer and the preaching of the Word come together. After many years of following Paul around, Timothy knew what he needed to pass on to his faithful men. Pastors who spend their time wisely in the Word of God and commit themselves to prayer will also know the kinds of things that need to be passed on to their group of leaders, as well as the regular church members.

Below is a suggested model[87] for addressing the lack of spiritual maturity often found in the local church today. It would be a great

---

[87]. These topics are taken from a series of booklets written by Dr. Sam Warren and presented in a training event called Pathway to Maturity. There are five book-

starting point for a pastor in spending time with his leaders. The ultimate goal would be for the group to reach a point where this relational process would be repeated in and through their own lives.

- **Christology**—When a person understands that Jesus Christ is the head of the church and receives its instruction from Him through the Holy Spirit, an attempt by man to assume that role is diminished. Not only is Jesus the head of the church, He is the creator of our world and all that is in it. Complete submission to His guidance is demanded for all believers.
- **Ecclesiology**—Once a follower of Christ accepts the role of Jesus Christ as the head of the church, they are in a position to understand and accept their proper role in the life of the church, His body. During this time, the follower of Christ will learn how they are gifted by God and able to discover their particular place within the body of Christ.

THE DEVELOPMENT OF A BIBLICAL WORLDVIEW

- **Emotionally Healthy Spiritually**—Dr. Peter Scazzero and his wife, Geri, have come to believe that it is impossible to become spiritually mature when one is *emotionally immature and unhealthy.* This is seen when one allows the lack of heath in areas of one's life to impact one's relationship with God and others negatively.

  Being in relationships built on trust a pastor can connect with his leaders at the deepest level. This type of relational intimacy can go a long way in achieving health among your leaders and ultimately the entire church body.

---

lets in this series: (1) *Effective Bible Study,* (2) *The Holy Spirit in the Life of the Believer and the Church,* (3) *Christology and the Believer,* (4) *Ecclesiology and the Believer,* and (5) *Pathway to Maturity: A Biblical Guide for Moving Believers to Maturity through the Local Church.*

- **Spiritual Gift Inventory**—Each believer engages in a journey to understand how God has specially gifted them to serve in and through the church. The believer is surrounded by those who know them and can affirm their giftedness.
- **4 Chair Discipling**—Training such as 4 chair discipling is one way to help the believer understand the relational process of moving a lost person and the new believer to becoming a fully devoted disciple that continues the relational process with others who come to faith.

  This model is a suggested path for any pastor who wants to take seriously the work of moving people toward spiritual maturity. It is a **curious thought** as to why this is not a common practice in the local church when one sees that many (if not most) churches have no plan for moving people toward spiritual maturity. The reality is that if you have no plan, **you do have a plan. It is a plan to fail.**

A pastor should not be overwhelmed with thoughts about beginning a fresh movement in his church that results in a new and exciting plan for making disciples. The following can serve as a simple guide for moving forward:

- Begin a private and personal commitment to praying for God's direction.
- Ask the Lord for at least TWO people to join you in this journey.
- Share with them the plan and seek a commitment to continue.
- Set the schedule. (Do not meet only when it's convenient.)
- Plan to journal throughout the process, noting things learned along the way.
- Every three months, reevaluate your progress. Take your time.
- At the end of the year, review and evaluate your progress. Determine how much longer you will commit to this original process.

- Pray for guidance as you set your disciples free to repeat the process with someone else.
- As pastor, begin the process again.

A Responsible and Accurate Evaluation of Progress

The church in Corinth was filled with controversy and accusations causing the Apostle Paul to question the spiritual status of many of the people. Prior to returning to the city and the church, he demanded that they take a close look at their lives:

> **Examine yourselves to see whether you are in the faith. Test yourselves.** Or do you not realize this about yourselves, that Jesus Christ is in you?—unless indeed you fail to meet the test! I hope you will find that we have not failed the test. But we pray to God that you may not do wrong-not that we may appear to have met the test, but that you may do what is right, though we may seem to have failed. For we cannot do anything against the truth, but only for the truth. (2 Cor. 13:5–8)

Few people like the idea of evaluation, but it is an absolute necessity for the church as we pursue maturity in the faith. We must find and/or create some way in which we can examine ourselves. Like Paul, we must take a careful look at our lives and not do anything against the truth (2 Cor. 13:7).

Below is a simple tool for conducting an evaluation of one's health status in regard to spiritual maturity.

AREA OF EVALUATION Describe the area under consideration as it pertains to your journey to become a healthy and fully devoted disciple of Christ.	PERSONAL EVALUATION GRADE Please rate yourself on the following scale: 5 = highest 1 = lowest
CLARITY *Do you have a clear picture of what is expected of you as a disciple of Christ?*	
HONESTY *As you evaluate your life according to the Bible's standards for being a disciple of Christ, are you being completely honest with yourself and others?*	
VULNERABILITY *Are you willing to allow others to speak into your life as you make your way to spiritual health?*	
TRANSPPARENT *Are you open to the scrutiny of others as they take a closer look at your life? Are you willing to put into action their suggestions?*	

Please describe the overall picture of your progress.

Final Thoughts

It may be necessary to wean oneself from other activities in order to do justice to the proposed plan and evaluation, but the fruit coming from this type of work will be incredibly valuable to you as a pastor or leader as you lead yourself and your people toward spiritual health.

CHAPTER STUDY QUESTIONS

STARTING WITH WHY

1. Consider asking one of your favorite businesses the what, how, and why of their existence.
2. What do you think the average passerby of your church thinks about what goes on inside the church?
3. Discuss your thoughts on the church as a group of people versus an organization. What is the main difference in your thoughts?
4. Consider the findings of Kinnaman and Lyons on the opinions non-Christians have of Christians. Why do you think their findings might be true?
5. Agree or disagree? Do you agree with the author when he says the WHY of the church is found in "we love because he first loved us" (1 John 4:19)? If so, why? If not, why?

STRATEGICALLY EQUIPPING

1. How important do you think preaching is in the growth of the church?
2. What do you think Paul meant when he said, "Take the sword of the Spirit, which is the Word of God" (Eph. 66:17)?
3. How does the Word of God *mend* those who hear it?
4. Do you believe that the pastor is the leader of the church and the key to the health of the church's future? If so, how?
5. In what way are the saints to be equipped for the work of the ministry?

TAKE ME TO YOUR LEADERS

1. Can a church misunderstand and misuse the key roles assigned to it ever expect to function as God intended?
2. How do you think the Bible distinguishes between elders and deacons?
3. Paul uses a familiar statement throughout the Pastoral Epistles. (This is a trustworthy statement.) What do think he means by this phrase and why?
4. What kind of leader was Timothy in the Ephesus church? What was his primary role?
5. Why do you think many churches have leaned toward a democratic approach to making decisions in the church? Do you think this is okay in light of the Scriptures?

THE TIMOTHY FACTOR

1. Check out Acts 16 to discover the reason Paul wanted Timothy to join him on his missionary journeys. What do you think it was?
2. How do you define godly? In what way was Timothy described in this way (2 Timothy 1)?
3. Timothy had an *unhypocritical faith.* How do you think Paul discovered this about his young apostolic delegate?
4. Discuss the following characteristics of a godly person found in the Pastoral Epistles:
    *   *Unhypocritical faith (2 Tim. 1:3–7)*
    *   *Unquestionable purpose (2 Tim. 1:8–9)*
    *   *Uncompromising process (2 Tim. 2:1–7)*
    *   *Unrelentless commitment (2 Tim. 3:8–13)*
    *   *Unending obedience (2 Tim. 4:1–8)*
    How important are these characteristics for today's leader?
5. Discuss the importance of putting into practice that which is preached in the church. Why is application so important to our spiritual growth?

PREACH THE WORD

1. Discuss the difference between *context* and *content questions*.
2. How important, in your opinion, is it to maintain *historical distance* in those situations where it is warranted?
3. Discuss the difference between *topical preaching* and *expository preaching* when it comes to equipping the saints for the work of the ministry.
4. How does storing up the Word of God in one's heart keep a person pure?
5. What do you think Paul meant in his advice to Timothy when he told him to "rightly divide the word of truth"?

JUST THE FACTS

1. What do you think Jesus meant when he called the twelve disciples that they might be **with Him**?
2. Why do you think so few churches today spend significant time making disciples?
3. How do you define a *disciple*?
4. How important is the humanity of Jesus to understanding how Jesus made disciples?
5. What are your thoughts about the ingredients of the *Description of a Discipled Person (DDP)*?

A BIG DO-OVER

1. Why would Billy Graham say that he would do things differently if he had to do it all over again?
2. Why do you think that Shackleton looked for men who could "shout a bit with the boys"? Do we need these kinds of people in the church?
3. What does it mean to abide in the vine? What about not to abide? How does one tell one from the other?
4. Have you ever yelled at the fruit and never looked at the nutrients?

5. Discuss the difference between conformation and transformation. What's the difference in the life of a follower of Christ?

THE MISSING PIECE

1. Do you think we have false teachers in the twenty-first century? How do you go about recognizing them?
2. Do you think the list given in 2 Timothy 3:1–5 is similar to the present-day world? If not, what's the difference?
3. How do you define the word *entrust* in terms of passing on the faith?
4. How important are relationships in the plan of Jesus as He calls us to make disciples?
5. Discuss the practice of prayer in the life of the church today. How healthy is it? Do we pray in the way that you see it talked about in the Scriptures?

THE BARE NECESSITIES

1. How have things been passed down to the next generation in your family?
2. Discuss the idea of passing only information to another person and calling it discipleship. What's wrong with this model?
3. What is sound doctrine? How is it passed on to the next generation?
4. Talk about WDJD instead of WWJD in terms of making disciples.
5. Discuss the biographical information on the twelve disciples. Are you surprised with those Jesus called to be with Him? If so, why?

A RECIPE FOR SUCCESS

1. When Jesus talked about the kingdom of God, what do you think He was referring to?
2. In John 17:4, Jesus said He had done what the Father gave Him to do. How did He know that He had done it?
3. Do you think there are things the church must do now like the first century church did to "save" themselves from the crooked generation? If not, what should the church do?
4. How important was the devotion of the early church to the Didache in keeping them safe?
5. Rate your church and its leadership in being able to...
    *   Understand the uncharted territory
    *   Leadership on the map is needed first
    *   Adaptation is everything off the map

Discuss the value of these three characteristics for a church that wants to move from the inside to the outside of their body. How will they make it possible for the church to reach the lost and lead them to Christ? Will this approach make it easier to get the job of making disciples as defined by Matthew 28:16–20?

BOOK SOURCES

- Intentional Disciplemaking by Ron Bennett
- Canoeing the Mountains by Tod Bolsinger
- The Training of the Twelve by A. B. Bruce
- How to Read the Bible for All It's Worth by Gordon Fee and Douglas Stuart
- The Never Alone Church by Dr. David Ferguson
- Tyranny of the Urgent by Charles Hummel
- The Making of a Disciple by Keith Phillips
- unChristian by David Kinnaman and Gabe Lyons
- Phillippa Lally, European Journal of Psychology
- Leading at the Edge by Dennis Perkins
- Lincoln on Leadership by Donald Phillips
- Real-Life Discipleship by Jim Putman
- Start with Why by Dr. Simon Sinek
- 4 Chair Discipling by Dr. Dann Spader
- Anatomy of a Revived Church by Dr. Thom Rainer
- People Fuel by Dr. John Townsend
- The Alexander Antidote by Dr. Sam Warren

OTHER SOURCES BY DR. SAM WARREN

- The Alexander Antidote: Turning Conflict into a Prescription of Wholeness for the Local Church
- Dead Men Talking: What Dying Teaches Us about Dying

ABOUT THE AUTHOR

Dr. Sam Warren writes from a position of experience. He has pastored for over thirty-five years, led a national and international ministry of leadership development, and now directs a consulting ministry to the local church (Far More Consulting, Inc.). Trained in the use of a variety of diagnostic tools to help the church, Dr. Warren uses these to assist the local church in becoming healthy as defined by the Scriptures. His previous books, *The Alexander Antidote: Turning Conflict into a Prescription of Wholeness for the Local Church* and *Dead Men Talking: What Dying Teaches Us about Living*, have been used to address common issues faced by the church as it carries out its ministry.

Dr. Warren lives in Jacksonville, Florida, with his wife of forty-five years, Shelly Ann Warren. Sam and Shelly have two grown sons, Jared and Darrick Warren.

In 2016, Dr. Warren started a Christian nonprofit consulting ministry for pastors, church leaders, and Christian nonprofit organizations. For more information, please contact or check out the following:

Website: Far More Consulting, Inc.
farmoreconsulting.churchspring.org
Email: warren2qxi@gmail.com
Mobile phone: 904-207-5196

CPSIA information can be obtained
at www.ICGtesting.com
Printed in the USA
BVHW070405091220
594980BV00003B/14